D. H. Lawrence's John Thomas and Lady Jane

According to

Spike Milligan

PART II of
Lady Chatterley's Lover

D. H. Lawrence's
John Thomas and Lady Jane

According to
Spike Milligan

PART II of
Lady Chatterley's Lover

MICHAEL JOSEPH LONDON

Thanks are due to the Estate of
Frieda Lawrence Ravagli

MICHAEL JOSEPH LTD

Published by the Penguin Group
27 Wrights Lane, London w8 5tz
Viking Penguin Inc., 375 Hudson Street, New York, New York 10014, USA
Penguin Books Australia Ltd, Ringwood, Victoria, Australia
Penguin Books Canada Ltd, 10 Alcorn Avenue, Toronto, Ontario, Canada m4v 3b2
Penguin Books (NZ) Ltd, 182–190 Wairau Road, Auckland 10, New Zealand

Penguin Books Ltd, Registered Offices: Harmondsworth, Middlesex, England

First published 1995
Copyright © Spike Milligan Productions Ltd 1995

Set in 12/14.5 pt Bembo by Datix International Ltd, Bungay, Suffolk
Printed in England by Clays Ltd, St Ives plc

A CIP catalogue record for this book is available from the British Library

ISBN 0 7181 3997 6

The moral right of the author has been asserted

D. H. LAWRENCE'S

JOHN THOMAS

AND LADY JANE

According to

Spike Milligan

PART II of

Lady Chatterley's Lover

Foreword

John Thomas and Lady Jane was the second of three versions of *Lady Chatterley*, all very different. It was given its title by the wife of Julian Huxley, who read the manuscript and was very cross morally, so she suggested, rather savagely, that it should be called this since, she said, these words were frequently used in the book for the male and female sexual organs. Strangely enough, Lawrence agreed. The words 'John Thomas' and 'Lady Jane' were, however, never used in the book (which leaves plenty of room for others that are a lot naughtier).

SPIKE MILLIGAN

Chapter I

OURS IS essentially a woeful age, so is eighty. So we refuse to take it woefully. The cataclysm has fallen and has been badly hurt in the fall. We have got to live no matter how many skies have fallen. Since records were kept the total number of skies that have fallen is 1,372. Having tragically rung our hands without them making a sound, we now proceed to develop a new species of duck with a quieter quack.

This was Constance Chatterley's position. She would spend long periods on her back. The war had landed her in a tight situation – gin did the damage.

She married Clifford Chatterley in 1917, when he was home on leave. They had a month's honeymoon when they hardly left the bed. Then he went back to the war to be wounded, and was shipped back over to England, more or less in bits. A parcel containing several fingers, an ear, and a nose was posted to his wife. His hold on life was marvellous. He did not die and the bits seemed to grow together again, except that his knees were at the back, so that he had to kneel backwards with his face behind him. He remained in the doctors' hands, then he was pronounced cured, and could return to life again, with the lower half of his body paralysed for ever. It was goodbye to screwing — for ever as well.

Clifford and Constance returned to the home of his family, Wragby Hall. His father, a general, had died in action — of bronchitis — for his country. They came to start housekeeping in the rather dilapidated home of the Chatterleys where the servants had to keep running away to avoid falling masonry. Clifford had no near relatives: they lived a half a mile away, but he had distant relations who lived in Australia and Canada. His brother, older than himself, was dead. He was screwing the wife of a French farmer when he shot him in the back. Crippled for ever, knowing he could never have any family, he came home with his young wife to keep the Chatterley name alive as long as he could. He started straight away and kept the name going all that day.

He was not downcast. He could wheel himself about in a bath chair, with a motor attached, that could do sixty miles an hour. At sixty mph in a wheelchair he could view all his estate in half an hour, having knocked down several of the estate workers on the way. He remained bright and cheerful: almost, one might say, chirpy, with his handsome face and his bright, challenging blue eyes. His shoulders were broad and strong, his hands were very strong, and the hairs on his chest were very very strong. But his dick was dead. He was expensively tailored, and wore very handsome neckties from Bond Street. He bought trousers bent at the knee to fit his legs.

He had so very nearly lost his life, that what remained to him seemed inordinately precious. He valued it at £500. One saw how proud he was of himself being alive, he and his sixty-mph wheelchair, and he could no longer feel anything from the waist downwards. He never knew whether he was wearing underpants or not, so Constance put a bell on them.

Constance, his wife, was a ruddy, country-looking girl with soft brown hair and sturdy body and slow movements full of unused energy. She had big, wondering blue eyes and big tits, and a slow soft voice, and seemed just to have come from her native village. This was not so – she had just come from Royal Ken-sing-ton. Her father was once a well-known Scots RA, Reid, but only once. Her mother had been an active Fabian, printing pamphlets accusing the Royal Family of standing in the way of progress. Between artists and highbrow performers, Constance and her sister Hilda had what might be called a cultured-unconventional upbringing. Seeing her in the streets people would say: 'Look, there goes a cultured-unconventional upbringing pair of girls.' They had been screwed in Paris, Rome, The Hague, and finally Berlin. These two girls were not in the least abashed, neither by art nor harangues, primarily because they were dim. They were at once cosmopolitan and provincial with high-brow provincialism and high-brow cosmopolitanism. One glance and people would, say:

'Look, there goes the cosmopolitan and provincial girls with their high-brow provincialism and high-brow cosmopolitanism.'

Clifford too had had a year at a university in Bonn, studying things connected with coal-mines, such as shovels, pick-axes, and hundredweight sacks. Because the Chatterley money had come out of coal royalties, Clifford wanted to be up-to-date, and for this effect every day he changed the date on his calendar. He was second son. It behoved him to give the family fortunes a shove if only he knew *where* they were.

In the war he forgot all that. His father, Sir Geoffrey, spent recklessly for his country. He would post small packets of bullets to the poor soldiers at the front. Take no thought for the morrow, for the morrow will take thought of itself. Well, this was the morrow of that day! Oh fuck, thought Clifford.

Clifford, first lieutenant in a smart regiment, knew most of the people in HQ and he was full of beans (he ate a tin every day). He liked Constance at once: first, because of her modest-maiden appearance, and of course her big tits. He managed to get the modern German books and he read them aloud to her. It's a pity she didn't understand a word. He had relatives 'in the know', and he himself therefore was in quite a lot of the same 'know'. It didn't amount to a great deal: about £10.

By the time the *Untergang des Abendlands* appeared, Clifford was a smashed man, trying to translate it took it out of him. It was the day after, the grey morrow for which no thought had been taken. He checked his calendar and sure enough it was the day after the grey morrow for which no thought had been taken.

Wragby was a low, long old house in brown stone, standing on an elevation and overlooking the bills and the reminders, on a long lease. There was a fine park beyond, one could see the tall smoking chimney and the spinning wheels of the colliery. But Constance did not mind this, she looked the other way. On some times when the wind blew west, which it did often, Wragby Hall was full of the sulphurous smell of burning pit-bank. For a while they thought it was the staff farting in concert.

She had never been used to an industrial district, only the Sussex downs, and Scotch hills, and Royal Ken-sing-ton, and other sufficiently aesthetic surrounds. Here at Wragby she was within the curious sphere of influence of Sheffield, the Valhalla of EPNS. If your cutlery wasn't stamped with it you were nobody. The skies were often very dark, there seemed to be no daylight, that's because it was night-time. There was always a faint or strong smell of some uncanny something: it was marmite. Wherever it was, on the breath one breathed in, and, yes, one breathed in marmite all day.

She had Clifford who would need her while he lived. After that he would have to fend for himself. She had certain duties to the parish. She made mince-pies for the Christmas sales, many of which were returned to her uneaten with dentures in them. Constance tried to get in touch a little with the miners'

wives. She wanted to know what the world was like
– it was round they told her.

Clifford would never go outside the park, in his
chair. He could not bear to have the miners stare at
him as an object of curiosity so Constance pushed
him under a blanket, which he looked out through
little holes in it. He could stand the Wragby servants.
Them he paid. But outsiders he could not bear. He
became irritable and queer and started having young
boys to tea. Poor Sir Clifford! Wounded in the war!
Poor Sir Clifford DSO – dick shot off.

The Duchess of Oaklands came and the Duke.
They tried to bolt the doors against them but they got
in through the scullery window and stayed for tea. It
was terrible.

'Thank God they've gone,' gasped Sir Clifford.

'Thank you, God,' said Constance. But she said they
were rather nice, a bit pathetic.

'A bit,' said Clifford. 'They were pathetic all over.
They drank eight pots of tea and ate every pastry in
the house. By Jove, Connie, your neck must be more
rubbery than mine if you could stand it.'

Constance couldn't stand it, she had to sit down.
The Duke and Duchess would hardly come again,
they were due to die next year. Of course there was
no real danger in Clifford. The marrow of him was
just as conservative as the Duke's own, whose marrow
had taken first prize in the country fair.

Clifford sometimes had his relatives on a short visit.
He would give them two hours to get out. He had
some extremely 'titled' relations on his mother's side

and a lot on his father's back. Clifford thought he was so democratic: he used 'bloody', 'bugger' and 'shit' in his poems. He still liked the fact that his aunt was a Marchioness, his cousin an Earl and his uncle, well he didn't know what he was, the failure of the family, a dustman. There were Chatterleys occupying prominent jobs in the government, the Ministries of Grit and Filth and exportable heads, good wires to pull, though Clifford couldn't pull his own. Sometimes Tommy Dukes came, he was a Brigadier General who was one of Haig's generals who managed to put a year on the war: the old Cambridge light, or another poet whose brief flower was blown.

> I wander lonely as a cloud
> That floats aloft o'er dales and hills
> When all at once I came upon
> A host of bloody daffodils.

His was good company to be in. They were BP. Usually when it wasn't some relation it was some lone man who smoked a pipe and wore strong brogue shoes.

But Constance and Clifford were a great deal alone. The months went by, even the years, no one could stop them. Clifford, with his eyes very wide open, bright and hard, and staring: he really needed glasses. He read a good deal though he wasn't profoundly interested in anything. That left nothing. He was interested in elephants, but he didn't have any. Constance made quaint drawings and illustrations for old books; sometimes her illustrations were published. Clifford was quite proud and always sent her books to titled relatives, titles like the Welterweight Champion of Wales and the Light Heavyweight Champion of London.

The great thrill of being alive began to wear off Clifford; it came off in handfuls. At first it had excited him terribly to be able to push his chair at sixty mph through the woods and see squirrels gathering nuts. If only he had a pair of his own. 'I'm alive, I'm alive,' he said and he sped off at sixty mph with Constance running beside him trying to keep up. If he heard a rabbit scream, caught by a weasel, his heart would stand still. 'Another one gone to death! Another one! And I'm still alive!'

Constance prayed that a giant weasel would come and put him out of his misery. He never betrayed his occupation with death to Constance but still she did not guess his strange, weird excitement when he took a gun in the autumn to shoot at his pheasants, the strange thrill he felt at banging away (something he couldn't do in bed), when he saw a bird ruffle in the air, and make a curving dive. When Constance objected he said, 'Look, the fall would have killed it!' He was acting very queer (if not to say gay). She tried to dissuade him from shooting. 'It's not good for your nerves and it is very bad for the birds.' And for a long time he would not touch his gun. Then some evening, frothing at the mouth, he would sit in a chair, sit waiting for a rabbit, or a bird, or a poacher – he often shot poachers. When he saw a thing fall dead, a puff

of exaltation exploded in his fart (sorry heart), and he
was proud of his aim, which he had trouble with
when urinating. He thought a great deal of the preser-
vation of his game though after three seasons' shooting
at Wragby there was hardly any left. He concentrated
on shooting poachers and became irritable and
strained. He would sit for a long time doing nothing,
he would do it in different languages – doing it in
French was not as good as doing nothing in German,
and best of all was doing nothing in Polish and
Mongolian.

'You know a lot about mining, Clifford,' said Constance. 'Couldn't you do something about the pits?'

'Everything will have to close down in the long
run,' he said. Constance had no intention of going for
a long run. 'We shall have to leave Wragby.'

To hear him like this chilled the life in her. She had
to put on a fur coat. He had a terrible fear of drowning
and wore a life belt. He was exacting about food. He
liked things exactly like food. He couldn't sleep and
that tortured him. He used to blame the Chinese.

Constance was silent and dogged, sometimes she
would bark. Clifford could never be a husband to her.
She lived with him like a married nun, and became a
virgin again by disuse. Their memory of one month
of married life became unreal to her. Mind you, they
did it so much it should have lasted a lifetime.

For the first few years. And then something began
to bend under the strain: it was her back. She began
to walk with a slight stoop, she became abnormally
silent and would start violently if addressed suddenly.

She shut sex out of her life and out of her mind. It was denied her so she despised it and didn't want it. But something was bending in her. It was her oesophagus that bent her food which started to go sideways. Some support was slowly caving in, she could feel it. She felt it every night, it was still there, in the morning she felt, 'now I'm getting up, now I'm washing myself, now I'm putting a dress on, now I'm going downstairs, now I'm opening Clifford's door, now I'm going to say good morning.' Like Domestos, she was going round the bend.

Chapter II

I T WAS HER father, Sir Malcolm, whom you will remember was once an R.A. He warned her. 'Look out,' he said. He was big, burly, beefy – he would have looked ideal on a butcher's block.

'Connie, I hope you're not putting too great a strain on yourself.' He could not stand his son-in-law, but then his son-in-law could not stand. Now he came after her with his queer Scottish persistency and a glass of malt whisky. Once a waiter in a restaurant asked if he wanted some ice in his malt and he said, 'Ice? Do you not know what it did to the *Titanic*?'

'You are not yourself Connie,' he said.

And she said, 'Then who am I? I'd love to know. I might be someone important.'

'You're running for a fall, the pair of you.'

'There isn't a pair of me,' she said, looking round.

'I find this house depressing in spite of your taste in arranging it. I count the hours until I can get out again.'

'Don't worry, I will count them for you.'

'It would be absurd, Connie, to ask you if you are happy,' he said.

'That's absurd of you to ask me that.'

'Would you say yourself you are happy? Perhaps you are not taking another thing into account.'

'What things do I have to take into account?'

'Yourself. You're screwing yourself.'

She wished he wouldn't keep saying 'screwing', that was just a memory.

'Well, you know I do not believe in screwing myself. Do you think I will collapse?' she asked.

'Why, decidedly I do! I am sure you will,' he said.

'What am I to do then to stop collapsing? Hurry, it might happen any minute.'

Their eyes met. He gave her one glance then turned aside. By walking round him she was able to meet it again. He hated Clifford, he loathed Clifford's special Englishy style, he always dressed on the left.

'What you need is more life, you need more enjoyment, you need younger people of your own age, you need to dance.'

Constance didn't tell him Clifford used to make her dance the Charleston naked and kept touching her with a feather duster which ruined her routine.

'Yes,' he said, 'you need to flirt a little, not too much, just a little squeeze of the boobs. Come away with me to the South of France for a month or two. Come, Connie, it will be best for you in the long run.'

Why, thought Constance, do people want me to do long runs?

Sir Malcolm had a second wife, a woman much younger than himself and with a much larger income, which he 'looked after' for her, and she went her own way and he went his. (He with a substantial sum of her money.)

She sighed and said, 'I can't leave Clifford in the winter.'

'Why not?' he said. 'He's got warm underwear. He can sit nearer the fire.'

As he had lived with her mother's obstinacy, he knew quite well when to give up. When you can do nothing with people you leave them to do things to themselves. Every night Constance took her clothes off and did things to herself. She looked up at him as he stood by the door drinking his third malt whisky and watched him walk into it.

'All right, Father!' she said softly. It was the quiet way his first wife used to speak to him – that, or 'Get out, you drunken bastard', but Connie was somehow softer, warmer, by about 3°F.

The meals with Clifford were always a trial. Clifford judged every dish. Clifford scrutinized the food in an intense way, using a jeweller's glass. Sir Malcolm hated eating at Clifford's table so he ate off the piano. The wine was white claret and he hated that. When he asked for a whisky and soda he felt the elderly butler begrudged it to him. With this refusal Sir Malcolm nearly had a seizure. There was a devastating sense of economy, especially in the drinks. The food was good and sufficient, Clifford noted on a piece of paper everything Sir Malcolm had and priced it accordingly and he would be served with the bill on his departure. When Sir Malcolm wanted a whisky and soda, a frosty tension was felt in the air. Constance broke the tension and said, 'I think my father would like another whisky and soda.'

The servants were all old servants of the family and Clifford had to put his will over theirs. The servants were his servants and had to follow his economies and they, poor people, couldn't help begrudging the whisky. It was one of his economical points. Simpson, the butler, elderly and grey and neutral who had been given notice thirty years ago, must, however, also begrudge the whisky. 'Look, Chatterley,' said Sir Malcolm, 'I will pay cash for it', and threw money on the table. And because of the tension Constance decided to leave.

Sir Malcolm lit up one of his cigars. He'd forgot to take off the cellophane wrapper and it flamed up. 'I don't think you know,' said Sir Malcolm taking his cigar from his mouth, 'that Constance is not getting altogether a fair show.'

Clifford went white with anger, purple with rage, and yellow with jaundice. 'I do not understand vague things like *fair show*,' said Clifford.

'Perhaps I was too vague. What I wish to say is that living a shut-up life as she lives here.'

'Is she shut up here?' asked Clifford. 'You keep telling too. I don't understand, I don't lock her in. She is unfortunate in being my wife, it is true.'

'I agree she is unfortunate in being your wife, by having to share the grievous misfortunes that have happened to you. If only the NAAFI tea urn had not been full when it fell on you.'

Another complete and lengthy silence. This time, one hour, Sir Malcolm was too astute to break the image of calm *bonhomie*. Crawling along the floor behind Clifford and with his back to Simpson, Sir Malcolm went to the drinks table only to find the whisky had a lock on it. He had to crawl back again. He shook his cigar ash in the fire but the tip of his nose was very white.[1]

'What kind of damage to Connie do you anticipate?' asked Clifford.

'Serious damage, her nerves will suffer, one of those illnesses that women get like leprosy, or consumption, malaria, swine fever, and are very often fatal. Where shall I get another drink?' asked Sir Malcolm holding his glass at arm's length in front of the butler. 'Look, I'll pay cash.'

'Oh,' said Clifford. 'Didn't he bring a tray?'

'No, he bloody well didn't.'

Clifford reached for the bell-push that hung on a cord on his chair, which wasn't connected to anything, but he did it. Simpson had reappeared with the tray. Then there was a hissing of soda-water, and Sir Malcolm took a large mouthful.

'And what remedy do you suggest?'

'I should like to put her on a course of iron jelloids, cod liver oil and Sanatogen and then a month in the South of France.'

[1] White — why?

'Well, if she wishes to go, she is perfectly free. I can start her off on the iron jelloids, cod liver oil and Sanatogen before she leaves.'

'Good,' said Sir Malcolm.

'Then,' said Sir Malcolm, coming to the point, 'she must know it is useless to wish for something there is no hope of ever getting.'

'What can she wish for that she has no hope of ever getting?' asked Clifford coolly. For a moment, he didn't realize how rash he was with a wilting willy.

'If you don't know that, I don't,' said Sir Malcolm, who had a prick as big as a dead eel.

The iron went right down into Clifford's soul. He had got into the habit of forgetting that Constance might have conjugal rights: or conjugal desires. Never mind, this course of iron jelloids, cod liver oil and Sanatogen might make up for it.

With that Sir Malcolm drank his seventh whisky and staggered out of the door. Clifford had the pleasure of hearing him fall from the top of the stairs to the bottom. He departed the first thing the next morning. Constance said she had been counting the hours for him until he left and it was twenty-three and a half.

Chapter III

IN THE LATE autumn, however, came a few very beautiful sunny days. Clifford roused himself to go out in his motor-chair. Constance had to run alongside to keep up. The soft, warm woolliness of the uncanny November day seemed utterly unreal to her in its thick, soft-gold sunlight and thick gossamer atmosphere. The park, with its oak-trees and sere grass, sheep feeding in silence on the slopes, and the near distance bluey, an opalescent haze showing through it the last yellow and brown of oak-leaves, seemed unreal, a vision from the past. What a lot of bollocks! It was an ordinary English autumn day.

The sun fell on the chair and the chair fell on Constance's foot.

He said to her, 'Would you like to sit down a bit and rest your injured foot? Constance, sit on yonder stump,' he said.

Connie sat on yonder stump and got an arse full of splinters.

'Who'll come here after us?' said Clifford looking into the distance.

Constance said: 'The way things stand, I would say the bailiffs.'

Constance looked around vaguely. The wood seemed as yet to hold some of the old inviolate mystery of Britain, even Druid Britain.[1]

'Perhaps we don't know what will come after us,' he said. 'Perhaps it will be quite different from what we expect. It could be small purple things.'

Yes, of course, small purple things. His tablets are wearing off, thought Constance.

Sometimes in the words she felt another influence, something mysteriously alive. What it was she didn't know, but it was mysteriously alive. But where was it? Wherever it was, it was mysteriously alive. She was becoming de-stabilized.

'I suppose the world will come to an end in its own way,' she said.

'I suppose so. Give me your hand.'

'Why? Will that stop the world coming to an end?'

As he grasped her hand she felt the life die out of her, ebb away, away from him, all her blood, which was Rhesus negative, seemed to recoil. Blood when it recoils can cause amnesia.

'You're lovely, Constance,' he said.

'Who are you?' she said, her blood recoiling.

'Wouldn't you like to see more people?'

---

[1] What a lot of bollocks!

'Who are you? More people? Yes, where are they?'
she said.

Where are they? expecting him to produce a crowd
for her.

Clifford apologized. 'Sorry, I'd need a little time to
assemble them,' he said.

'Who are you?' she said, still with recoiling blood
amnesia.

'Would you like to go away for a while?' he asked.

She was silent for a time, by his watch it was one
minute and fifty seconds.

'Why?' she insisted.

'For your health. I'm afraid you might get depressed
and get swine fever.'

'No, since I've been on iron jelloids, cod liver oil
and Sanatogen I don't get depressed, I just get the
shits. What would be the good of going away?' she
said. 'I should only think of you all the time.'

'And I should think of you,' he said. 'There you'd
be in France thinking of me — and I'd be in Great
Britain thinking of you. Wouldn't that be exciting?'

She was silent, her hand lay dead in his, he buried it.

'Tell me, what would be the good of my going?'

'Perhaps you need to enjoy yourself, like the
women at the night clubs. Perhaps you need to jazz and
flirt and perhaps have men make love to you or some
man. I can't do it. To me it isn't a necessity.'

'You mean you don't mind if I let a man fall in
love with me?' she said.

'It's no use my minding. If you are going to go to
pieces or have a mysterious malady like swine fever, I

pray to God some man will fall in love with you quickly; an hour should do it.'

'You don't mind if there were a child?' she said adding to his torment. His other torment was piles. 'You don't think you might lose me to one of the men who is in love with me?'

'I suppose it is one of the risks I will have to run,' and that was the last thing he could do: run.

'I'd try not to,' she said softly.

He gave a quick cracked laugh. Agahh – crackle! Agahh – crackle! Agahh – crackle!

She took the opportunity to rush upstairs and change. She patted her fanny and said, 'Help is on the way'. Returning she said, 'I don't really want to leave if you do not want me to.'

'Maybe not,' he said. 'There are things more powerful than sex. Right now I can't think of any. Whatever they are they go much deeper. For instance whales go much deeper.'

Whales. His tablets were wearing off. 'Sex is only an incident, just like dinner.' Nonsense, no one could live long without dinner.

'Probably you don't want to leave me for a sexual love or dinner.'

She heard it very distinctly. Here was her chance of a fuck. Was it coming closer? She had not betrayed anything if whales were deeper than their love, so be it. They were both moved.²

Out of a cross riding just below where they sat, a

---

² He had moved to the fireplace and she to the piano.

spaniel dog came towards them as if he had smelled their emotions from afar. It must have been very strong, he lived a mile away. She ran towards them, uttering a soft, suppressed little bark.

'Come here then little doggy,' said Constance releasing her hand from Clifford's and holding her hand out to the dog – it bit her.

Out of the riding came the gamekeeper dressed in greenish velveteen corduroy and a big hat. He looked appalling, like a scarecrow on the moors. 'Oh, I say, Soames,' said Sir Clifford, seeing his red face like a bum with a rash on it.

'Sir?'

'Turn my chair around for me and get me started. It makes it easier for me, Soames.'

'You want me to get you started or the chair?' Soames was a great thinker.

Soames came striding up the slope with a quick small movement, slinging his gun over his shoulder. It missed, and fell in the mud. He was of medium build, his face was of medium build with vermilion-ruddy colour, he looked like a weather report. He had a rather large sticking-out brown moustache. His bearing had a military erectness and resistance. He was silent, it hurt his brain to talk, his movements were soft, silent, oafish, almost secretive and evasive. He could be an outrider for MI5, and if so they were desperate for recruits.

The man touched his hat to Constance. He also touched his trousers, sleeves and socks. 'Shall yer manage for yerself, or should I wheel you?' he asked in a harsh, neutral voice with a local accent.

'Perhaps you'd better come along and give her a bit of a push up the park incline.'

So Soames pushed Lady Chatterley a bit up the park incline. Clifford had referred to the wheelchair but Soames MI5 had misunderstood the hidden message in Clifford. The man turned to close the gate and Constance let him. She bent and patted the dog which wagged its tail before it bit her again.

'Sorry about that, marm,' and he kicked the dog up the arse.

Constance came on a little up the rear, aware of Clifford's face glancing around to see where she was and she was exactly where she was.

The gamekeeper pushed the chair with a slow, deliberate step taking his foot lingeringly from the ground. Constance liked the colour of his appalling greenish velveteen corduroys with fawn cloth leggings. What a strong back the man had! What she did not know was that Soames, by pushing the chair, had ruptured himself. Since she had got used to the Derbyshire-Yorkshire dialect of the people round Wragby, she found other dialects, like the hill tribes of Assam and the Cocos Keeling Islands, distasteful. Since his wife had left him, Soames had lived quite alone in the cottage in the woods. Clifford liked him because he was a good keeper, did not drink or smoke, but he was a compulsive onanist. Every morning he had to break his blankets. He was a man nearing forty but he wasn't speeding. During the war his wife had gone loose, so loose bits used to fall off her. She would entertain men down in the cottage to the disgust of the old Sir Geoffrey, only because he wasn't in on it. She used to do a dance, 'Isadora Duncan and the Dance of the Seven Veils', using surplus army blankets to the disgust of old Sir Geoffrey because *he* wanted to do it – he wanted to entertain men in the cottage. She had gone off to Stacks Gate and that was the end of her.

Soames was apparently a cruel man. He would put mustard on cats' arses and watch it set off. Constance herself did not care for his harsh tenor voice that had a peculiar clanginess. 'Good morning – clang – Your Ladyship – clang,' he would say. He had a soft furtiveness of his movements as if he were hiding himself, this he did behind trees. She watched the slow, sensitive way he lifted his feet and put them back on earth again. He had to, he lived there. She realized something, he was alone. Well, she couldn't see anybody else. It was no good Clifford talking to her about lovers. She could no more have a score of lovers than a tiger cat can. Tiger cats have 100 matings a year; each one lasted half an hour, and for her it was too late. It had nearly gone six o'clock, much too late to start mating. She didn't want people, she wanted to draw away from them more and more. Drawing away by walking backwards she ended up eighteen miles away in the wheat field in the park. Living a life meant avoiding people, the best way to avoid people was go round them. And yet she did want – as even a tiger cat wants a mate, though the mate will probably devour his offspring. She would never mate with a man who would eat their children.

Clifford had waited for her at the top of the slope, by his watch one hour and twenty minutes. The day was already drawing to a close. He was drawing to a close. The damp mist was beginning to close up. It closed up on Clifford and you could not see him, just his head stuck out of the top of the mist. An infinite saddened melancholy seemed to settle over the park, mostly over Clifford. Clifford's little motor-chair puffed with a forlorn, waiting puff.

'You're not feeling tired, are you?' he asked, his head poking out of the mist.

'Oh no,' she said and said no more. She was aware of the keeper looking at her and she glanced at him. His eyes were light brown, hers were blue, Clifford's were grey, the dogs were grey and Lloyd George's were hazel. Soames had eyes with tiny black pupils, like any of London's schools. Soames looked at her eyes, they were full of indescribable trouble, his were full of conjunctivitis. He had realized that she was a young woman alone out of her depth, drowning – should he alert the coastguard? Again he met the strange dark turmoil of her eyes, the look of one who was drowning.

Yet she was well off. She had everything she wanted – clean underwear every day with the stains removed, champagne and frogs' legs for breakfast, except her husband was paralysed. Well, other women had to live with their men who were paralysed, plenty of women had lost their husbands. She should be thankful for what she had got. As a character analysis it wasn't bad for a gamekeeper.

Nevertheless, something kept stirring. He had kept himself without feeling for a long time now, although occasionally he would feel himself at night. Feeling was finished with him with the war. Before the war he had felt himself all over every day to see if he was still there. Some people said he wasn't all there. Let everybody keep their feelings to themselves, especially the women. The war had been bad. The women had been worse. Women worse than the First World War, that couldn't be right. Women made things so much worse, they couldn't boil a four-minute egg. Six, eight and ten minutes, yes. After all, Lady Chatterley had drawn a blank in the marriage lottery. Sir Clifford was all right but not enough balls to him. Actually he had enough but they were neutralized. But that was apparently what women liked, men with their balls neutralized.

They came to the house, Clifford was helped into his indoor chair from his outside chair by Marshall who was gardener and husband to the housekeeper.

'Thanks for the help, Soames,' said Clifford. 'Good night!'

'Yer welcome, Sir Clifford!' came the harsh, hard voice.

'Oh good night!' said Constance's voice, soft and startled.

'Good night, Your Ladyship!' came distinct and colourless.

He turned away and made his way home, him and his silk white body and holding his rupture in place with his right hand.

Chapter IV

AS THE LAST days of autumn fell into the gloom of winter, Constance took as little heed as possible. Some days she took no heed at all. She had trained herself to be unconscious to the English weather while she was. To bring her around the maid threw an occasional bucket of water over her. In the old days they had always gone abroad for the worst months. Even at home it was not quite so bad near the downs. They had stayed at terrible Bexhill-on-Sea, an above-ground cemetery.

She followed the women's rule of keeping herself in order by maintaining a strict rhythm in the house, one day they all did the Foxtrot, one day it was the Charleston, and one day it was the Black Bottom. She kept a watch on the vegetable garden, it kept perfect time. She kept busy by making curtains, carpets, cupboards, tables, chairs and bows and arrows for the poor of Africa. She could find no real joy in anything except in making curtains, carpets, cupboards, tables, chairs and bows and arrows for the poor of Africa.

She disciplined herself without relenting. Yet she knew in herself that it was dead. Instead of lying dead, she was walking about doing things, she was very lucky to be dead and walking about. She hired a coffin and spent part of the day lying in it. In her state it's a wonder she didn't consider being buried.

This was Constance's condition, she was dead and making curtains, carpets, cupboards, chairs, tables and bows and arrows for the poor of Africa. Oh! I want my heart to open. If ever there was a case for open-heart surgery, she was it. Oh, if only God or Satan or a policeman would help me to open my heart, I can't open it to Jesus. He too is dead, he's too much like Clifford. Rubbish! Jesus could use his legs to walk on water. Was there nothing she could open her heart to, like a blood bank? Sometimes, through her sleep, she would wake feeling strange and she felt herself and she would feel strange. On such a day she came down and saw Clifford. Oh how miserable and despicable he was.

'Oh how miserable and despicable I am,' he said.

Her mood was on her like an insanity and she could not shake it off. She shook and shook and yet it would not come off. She would show the world, she would stop making curtains, carpets, cupboards, tables, chairs and bows and arrows for the poor of Africa. They would have to get on without her. It seemed to her that something ghastly and deadly blew from the North Pole. And there was a stranglehold of death-breathing air. She saw it in the household staff. Yes, the death-breathing air was getting into the servants,

she could see it go in and come out a different colour
at the back. And on the awful corpse-days the sheep
huddled and hopped. (Sheep don't hop, they must
have been kangaroos.) She loathed sheep. Pigs were
poetic in comparison.

> Oh pig oh pig
> You really are big
> Yet you don't give a fig
> The pig – I dig.

She was like the earth in Labrador. Why? It was a
puzzle because she didn't look anything like the earth
in Labrador. She didn't even look like the earth in
Bexhill-on-Sea.

On one of her bad days she hurried out to walk
alone in the woods. In the distance she heard the
report of a gun. Why must some fool of a man be
letting off a gun at that hour? Perhaps it was Clifford
killing a poacher. She walked on oblivious to everything – oblivious to the Statue of Liberty, the Arc de
Triomphe, and Bexhill-on-Sea. She didn't know how
far she had gone. She heard a child crying, sobbing;
someone was illtreating a child. Down a narrow path
she saw two figures, a little girl in a purple coat and
moleskin hat. Soames in his terrible velveteen corduroys bending over her, saying:

'Shut it up, now, shut it up! Enough on it! If Ah
dunna kill 'im, 'e kills th' bods an' th' rabbits. Are ter
goin' ter stop it, eh?' With that he put his gun to the
child's head.

Constance strode nearer with blazing face, eyes and neck, nose and teeth.

'What's the matter? Why is she crying?' demanded Constance. 'Don't you dare kill that child.'

His eyes narrowed for the moment, then they slitted into slits. He did not deign to answer but looked into Constance's blazing face, eyes and neck, nose and teeth.

'Yo' mun ask 'er!' he said, curt and decisive. 'And if she gives the wrong answer she gets it.'

Constance started as if he had smacked her in the face.

'I asked you, you slit-eyed swine!'

'Ay! Ah know yo' did! But 'er's none towd me why 'er's scraightin', so 'appen yo'd better ax 'er.'

What in God's name was the oaf saying? She turned her back on him and crouched before the child.

'What is it, my dear? What has he done to you?'

'It's the pussy!' came in shaking tones.

'What did he do to your pussy?' said Constance.

''E shot it there!' she said.

'What did he shoot your pussy for?'

'I don't know.'

'Yi that does!' came the derisive, contemptuous voice of the man. 'Tha'rt a little liar.'

'You brute, swine, scum, murderer, rapist and serial pussy-cat killer!' she said. 'She was sorry for the cat.'

'There's the cat! There! If anybody wants to be sorry for him!' And stretched out in the brambles lay a large, rusty black moggy with a big head and amazing flat flanks. He had so much buckshot he looked like a cribbage board.

Constance and the child went off down a narrow path leaving the man, his gun, his dog and a dead cat. What a romantic tableau. They walked slowly away feeling they had scored which was more than the English football team.

They arrived at the cottage, the door was open.

'Look, Gran, what the lady gave me!'

She held out a sixpence. The grandmother snatched it out of her hand and put it in her purse. 'And what do you say?'

'Thank you,' said the child.

'Thank you, *Your Ladyship*. You know what your father said, don't you?'

'Yes. Stop crying, you little bastard!'

'Bye bye,' said Constance, laughing and backing away.

Constance continued to walk away till she was out of earshot, not that anybody would want to shoot her ear at that time of night. That man had been so insolent, insolent, brute, swine, bastard, murderer, rapist and serial cat killer.

And back in the woods Soames had buried the cat. The dog had dug it up and was dragging it down the path down the hill.

It was very soothing to sit and hear Clifford reading aloud, 'Humpty Dumpty sat on a wall, Humpty Dumpty had a great fall.' His voice was cultured, he read well and was wearing a schoolboy cap. Clifford wanted to send a message to the gamekeeper – logs for the winter.

Constance needed a walk. Among the trees was depth within depth of untouched silence, as in an old, yet virgin forest – the only virgin in the area.

When she came to the gamekeeper's cottage there was no one there. Rubbish, *she* was there. Constance knocked – no one came. She knocked again, she peeped through the window, she knocked again but no one came, she knocked again, still nobody came. There were no people, only one who was knocking at the door. She went tippy-toe around the cottage, happily knocking as she went. She was sure that there was nobody.

Then suddenly into a little gateway she stopped as if she had been shot. There was Soames washing himself. She knocked on him but he did not answer. He wasn't in. He had stripped to the waist, his awful velveteen breeches sagged low on his hips. And he was ducking his head repeatedly into the warm soapy water, rubbing his hands over his brown hair and over the reddened back of his neck.

Constance knocked on him again but he did not answer. The white torso of the man seemed so beautiful to her. Oh why oh why didn't he lower his trousers? The white, firm, divine body with its silky ripple and white arch of life, as it bent over the water. She couldn't help it. In all the world of gods she had got the hots for him. The silky firm skin of the man's body glistened broad on the dull afternoon. Oh why didn't he lower his trousers? Never mind who he was, never mind what he was, she had seen beauty and beauty alive. Oh fire in the fanny. That body smelling of Sunlight soap was of the world of the gods, cleaving through the gloom like a revelation. She felt again there was god on earth, but why, oh why, didn't he lower his trousers?

A great soothing came over her heart along with the feeling of worship. A sudden sense of pure Sunlight soap beauty, beauty that was active and alive, and shooting cats had put worship in her heart again. It was free-fall fanny! Not that she worshipped the man or his body but worship had come to her because she had seen a pure loveliness that was alive and that had touched the quick in her. Fanning the flame came the smell of burning pubic hair. It was as if she had touched god and had been restored to life. The broad, gleaming whiteness. Perhaps if she hurried back he would have lowered his trousers.

That he was a serial cat murderer did not matter any more. She knew he was only a gamekeeper, that did not matter. He did not own his own body. That was owned by the Bradford & Bingley. Were all men like that? Had Clifford been like that? No, Clifford would never stoop to wash in hot soapy water with Sunlight soap, with his trousers round his waist. No, Clifford had been handsome and well made but there had been something clayey or artificial in his body. No, not that silky quick shimmer and power, the real god-beauty that has no clay, no dross! Clifford had never been like that. There had always been some deadness in his flesh. A chiropodist had seen to that.

She stood on the threshold of the cottage. She knocked and then she heard him coming down the stairs. When he opened the door she was there on the threshold and he still had his trousers up. He stood there in a clean shirt. He had on a Sunday necktie of shot silk. He had shot it himself in the woods. Did he really have that white, curving lovely body she had seen? No, she had imagined it. He was what his face was: an ugly bastard.

'Lord Chatterley wanted some logs for the winter.'

'All right, my lady! I'll see to all the things that Sir Clifford wants.' Like legs he thought.

She felt him looking after her, as she departed. He would be thinking something stupid and mean she thought. He wasn't, he was thinking he would like to give her one. The hidden loveliness of his body, even if it were there under the flannelette shirt, was not his. No, it belonged to the Bradford & Bingley and the beautiful body of a man who was going away from them. He had given her such pleasure, she got pleasure out of Beethoven Symphonies and from some pictures of the site of Florence in the sunshine or Doris in the moonlight but ah, that gamekeeper's body.

As for sex, what she had known of it – and she had had brief experience of other men, about thirty – not a bad score, before Clifford. Some had big ones but Clifford didn't have one at all. Even her father knew that.

The man's body – ooooh! It seemed to live in itself – ooooh! Some people's bodies live in the Dorchester.

He found his body more economical living in a cottage. Perfect, powerful, hidden, godly, apart from the man who was vulgar and shot cats. The man's mind and his spirit were crude, uninformed, vulgar. His body alone was a lovely plunging thing, divinely living on – oooooh knickers! It was beauty that rippled and made quick movements – oohhh knickers! and was dangerously alive, no cat was safe near him, curving in the white arch of life. Oh, Oh, Oh, God help me! Clean knickers, please.

She listened to Clifford reading. He had found an old copy of the second part of *Hajji Baba*. When Constance went to bed she did something she hadn't done for some years. She took off all her things and looked at herself naked. She did it almost without thinking and without knowing what she was looking for. She soon found it smothered in pubic hair, she knew she was supposed to have a good figure – £10,000. She had a certain fluid proportion, she leaked. Her limbs were rather soft and slow. She had to wait for them. In the ripening of the warm fullness, her body was like a fruit, still greenish like unripe bananas. Yes, that was it, her body looked like an unripe banana. Her breasts were sinking. Should she call out the lifeboat? She twisted to look at her back. She looked at the beautiful sloping hips and buttocks. Like long yellow grapes! Like hillocks of sand as the Arabs say, long, soft and downward slipping. God help her! Her body was slipping down. She struggled to hold it up. Was the bloom gone and the delicate contour, while still it was a green fruit? No, no no, it

was like unripe bananas. She went to bed in despair.
She wept the first tears she had for many a long time.
She had to wring out the pillow.

Chapter V

CHRISTMAS WAS near, the day of dread. It was on that day in the war that Clifford had suffered his wounds. A choir came to the door and sang 'Jingle Bells', 'God Rest Ye Merry Gentlemen' and 'The Twelve Days of Christmas'. To all this he shouted, 'Fuck off'. 'Merry Christmas,' they shouted to him. 'Fuck Christmas,' he said.

Constance sent word for the keeper to bring a few branches to the house along with a few brace of pheasants. Constance went down with her unripe banana body and there was a huge black and scarlet bunch of holly and long brown-gold lines of pheasants' tails. It gave her a sense of ripeness and wildness, the latter having been specially killed for Christmas, and full of lead shot which would poison the guests.

'Splendid,' said Constance. 'Splendid. That is beautiful.'

She bent to stroke his dog; it bit her. He gave a quick salute and seemed to melt from the kitchen.

There were only five guests: her husband's aunt,

Lady Eva, Olive Strangeways and her husband Jack, Tommy Dukes and Harry Winterslow. Olive and Jack had come for Clifford's sake. Olive had always had a *tendre* for Clifford and dozens of other men. Lady Eva belonged to one of the very titled families, but was slightly in disrepute because of her gambling and her brandy. Tommy Dukes, the Brigadier General, who ordered a three-mile retreat when in fact the troops were advancing. He was fond of Clifford, and he was very good company. Witty, amusing, dry, original, he spoke fluent Arabic. It was a complete waste of time because no one else did. Everyone else spoke a second language of German, a third language of Czech and a fourth language of Swahili. Nobody understood each other for the whole evening.

Harry Winterslow was the General's friend. He used to help him get his cat out of the tree. It was very simple — he shot it. He wrote poetry that Constance could not understand.

> High cobalt sky
> The rooks caw
> Oh how the night throbs
> I must feed the wolves.

In fact, nobody understood it.

This left Jack Strangeways more or less alone. They did this by locking him in his room. So Jack made up to Connie through the keyhole. He was like many young people after the war. He was a neo-conservative and a neo-aristocrat and skint.

Suddenly Clifford said, 'My God, if ever we get a revolution in England, how I should love to charge the rabble with machine-guns, shouting "Long live the King".'

Constance felt like kicking him so she kicked him. 'What rabble?' she said.

'Those damned bolshevist-socialist lot,' he said. 'Look at Russia.' So they all looked at Russia.

Then they looked at Lady Eva, her nose reddened with brandy into a storm of veins. She was a pathetic instance of not being able to love anything. She couldn't do it any more. She had done it until she was sixty then it had healed up.

Lady Eva said, 'If civilization needs no love, we might easily become a bee-hive community.'

'Even that requires a queen bee,' said Dukes quietly.

'And what woman could lay 3,000 eggs?' said Jack.

'If I know anything about human nature, we will become an ant-heap and soon a big ant-eater will come along and lick it up with a curly tongue,' said Tommy Dukes softly.

'How nice,' said Olive. 'And what then?'

'Ask the ant-eater,' said Jack.

Olive caught the next train to London, took a taxi to Whipsnade Zoo, found the ant-eater's cage and asked him, 'If we all turn into ants would you come along and lick us up?'

It didn't answer so she caught the train back to Wragby Village and said to Jack, 'What a bloody fool you were to ask me to ask the ant-eater. I asked him four times and he didn't answer. You are a bloody fool.'

'People say all women are materialists,' he said sarcastically.

'You're wrong,' said Lady Eva. 'I know women who are anything but materialists. Mrs Aida Gooks.'

'Who's she?'

'She's a woman who is anything but materialistic.' Lady Eva and her nose took a sip of brandy. 'Mrs Eileen Veg.'

'Who's she?' said Dukes.

'She's another woman who is anything but materialistic.'

'Would you dance with me?' said Lady Eva. 'I love to Foxtrot.'

'I should like it more than I can say,' he replied. So he didn't say it.

'We'll manage better with music, Lady Eva.'

'Much better!' She started to sing a Foxtrot. 'Barney Google with the goo-goo Googley eyes.'

Connie had to dance with fat Jack.

Why did fat Jack have that funny thread of hate for women? Constance didn't know that he was one of London's leading homosexuals.

Connie knew this when he was dancing with her. He held her hand lightly, but kindly, and his arm against her shoulder had a certain protectiveness in its guidance. Essentially he was a thousand miles away from her so she was very lucky to have him in the room with her.

Chapter VI

CHRISTMAS WAS over, the guests were gone. They had talked volumes of utter crap. Clifford seemed irritable, now the excitement of the strangers had passed. Of her existence he was strictly unaware. She had to see a map to remind her where she was but there was little or nothing to hope for except a good screw.

As it was, they were nothing, and they had nothing to draw upon except an exercise-book. Clifford collapsed completely and merely lay in bed covered in ash – it blew in from the mines. Clifford lay in bits all over the floor.

No life came in to her and what life she had oozed out all over the floor. She began to get thinner. When she came into the room people would say, 'Where are you?' There was a pulse in her neck which could be seen shaking. When she looked into the mirror her head appeared to be jumping up and down. Energy flowed into her, from the sources: Daddy, HP and Tomato.

In six weeks she was a changed creature. For a while she became a frog. Her golden-ruddy colour had gone earthy. She was now brown. She had never been thin in her life. She rubbed her thin arms and thin thighs. She rubbed them and rubbed but they never got any fatter.

At last she wrote to Hilda. 'I haven't been well lately, and seem to have gone very thin and turned into a frog, but I don't know what's the matter. As yet I haven't met any frogs I fancy.'

Hilda at once prepared to descend on Wragby. When she saw Constance as a frog she said, 'Connie, what's the matter?'

Constance said, 'I don't know.' She showed her one thin arm and then showed her the other thin arm and it was just as thin.

'But you are really thin, what do you imagine it is?'

'I don't know.'

Hilda went to interview Clifford and found him remote, irresponsive, also dead. He was just waiting for the coffin.

'What's the matter with Constance, Clifford? She's gone so terribly thin and she has turned into a frog.'

'Oh, that's her trying to get sympathy.'

'I don't see how a frog can get sympathy. I think we had better find out.' Hilda insisted she should be taken to London to Hilda's own doctor. 'We will only be away one night, Clifford. You don't mind?'

'I hate being alone!'

'You *must* have a nurse,' said Hilda.

'I don't want a nurse. I've had enough of nurses.

The last one I had was during the war, it was a knee-trembler in a doorway.'

'When you've worn Constance out so that she can do nothing for you, what will you do then? You are not a cheerful man.'

'I'm a cripple, you expect me to be cheerful with a frog for a wife?'

'You will *have* to *have* a nurse.'

Hilda put a frog on the doctor's table. 'I see she has had a personality change,' he said. 'She is living too much off her reserves and now she's got no reserves. She must get away and take her mind off things. If she doesn't, I can't answer for the consequences.'

'What sort of consequences?' Hilda insisted.

'Her mother died of cancer, didn't she? These things start out of some depression, or repression which lowers the vitality. The fact she's a frog shows me stress and strain, but she will soon be back to her old self.'

'We had better get a nurse for Clifford,' said Hilda. 'Perhaps we can get Mrs Bolton.'

Mrs Bolton was a widow, good-looking in a quiet way. If you put your ear to her, you couldn't hear a sound. Clifford agreed. He hated giving himself into strange hands. She had not got strange hands. 'They were perfectly normal,' said Constance.

Mrs Bolton was glad of Lady Chatterley's offer. She had got tired of humping miners up the mine-shaft to the surface.

'Yes, I have known Sir Clifford since he was a tiny

toddler, and a lively one he was. He used to put firecrackers under cats' tails.'

It was obvious she did not like Sir Clifford. Whenever she got a chance she tried to push his wheelchair over the cliff. She did not believe the upper classes had any heart. The upper classes didn't have them. What they did have was frogs' legs and Champagne for breakfast.

So Ivy Bolton appeared at Wragby. For the first two days she was very nervous: she hid under the piano. She was extremely circumspect and subdued. But now she couldn't say fuck off to miners. Clifford let her do things for him though his resentment amounted to hatred of her. He tried to bite her tits through her dress. She kept very quiet, never trying to command him, for his own good, as she did the colliers. 'Bring a hundredweight of coal, you bastard, and put it down my coal hole.' Those days were gone. She kept herself quiet and mysterious. She dressed as a fortune-teller for the first week and hid under the piano. Grey eyes downcast, like this she used to walk into walls.

'Shall I do this, Sir Clifford, or would you rather I didn't bother.'

'Do you mind if we leave it for an hour or so?'

'Yes, Sir Clifford.' One hour later she poured out stone-cold tea.

Constance went, and the house took on a new rhythm. Before her the servants had lived way off. Now they seemed to come nearer, a little too near. Clifford woke to find his manservant in bed with him.

Mrs Bolton helped Clifford to bed at night. She put on his pyjamas and saw his poor, shrunken willy, and she crossed herself. All the heavy, intimate jobs that had fallen to Constance now fell to her, like giving Clifford a piggyback to the bathroom. Clifford never any more felt closeness to Constance. He would on occasions ask her to strip and do the Charleston.

Clifford, on his way to total lunacy, had mystical experiences, sort of exaltations and experience of identification with the One. Constance mistrusted these experiences: who was the One? But he insisted on the necessity for everyone to have the mystical experience of identification with the One. Who was the One? Was it anyone she knew – it seemed to him like pure Light – and to bring this experience with them down into life.

With the One it seemed that he insisted that *he* was the One – the great I am. Mrs Bolton knew nothing of it. Mrs Bolton would not give him a piggyback any more even if he was the One. As the One he read Plato's *Phaedrus*.

The Phaedrus myth had a certain fascination for her, that is, she didn't understand it. True, she didn't care about the progress of the soul, nor the Truth, nor the knowledge, nor the Philosophers' heaven. She was perfectly satisfied with Bexhill-on-Sea. All she wanted was a good shag. He asked her to undress and do an encore of the Charleston.

'Oh Clifford! Look at you. How dead you are.'

Clifford looked at himself and saw how dead he was.

'Can I put my clothes on? I'm getting cold.'

'Oh yes,' he said. We know what a woman is after. The thing is he couldn't give it to her.

She went to her room before Mrs Bolton came. Why drag out the evening with him? At last she was in rebellion. She stamped her foot on the floor, displacing the light fitting on the ceiling below.

A late day in March Mrs Bolton said, 'Why don't you take a walk through the woods, my lady, and look at the daffodils?'

'I give up, why don't I take a walk through the woods and look at the daffodils?'

For a long time she thought of the cottage. It was the vision of his cottage, the dark cottage on a dark, lonely winter afternoon. That gave her the queer burn on her heart. Yes, she had heart-burn, but she took Gaviscon for it.

And she felt stronger. She could walk better though she was still weak. The world was alive! 'Thou hast conquered, O pale Galilean!' – But there was to be a resurrection. Clifford was waiting to ride into heaven on his wheelchair. But there was to be a resurrection, the earth, the animals and men. One day we would see elephants, horses and men ascending into heaven. She wanted live things, animals, birds, stoats and rabbits, hawks and linnets, deer, wolves, lambs, foxes. That was enough for the time being.

She went slowly across the park. Her speed was about three miles per hour. It was a blowy day and she felt weak. Several times she was blown over. But the sunshine blew in sometimes and the wind blew up

her dress and up her knickers, causing her acute agita-
tion. She was glad to flee into the woods, like a
stricken thing, and hid in a bush to avoid an attack
from a centaur.

Wild daffodils fluttering as the wind pounded. Poor
little things. Perhaps they liked it! Perhaps they remember the war when the Zeppelins bombed England.
Yes, perhaps they were bombed. Poor little things. It
was too much, she started to cry, poor little thing.
She was tired and for a while she only walked on one
leg.

The hut was in the hidden place among the trees. It
was here the pheasants were resting and when the
time came, Clifford would blast them from the sky.
The brown dog came running towards her. She held
out her hand and the bastard bit it. She saw the keeper
in his shirt-sleeves bent over one of the chicken coops.
She approached slowly, her limbs melting as she did
and they lay in pools on the ground. She felt so weak
and breathless. He looked at her and seeing her so thin
and so lost-seeming, something stirred in his bowels –
it was the porridge he'd had for breakfast.

'Shall yer sit i' th' hut a while?' he asked.

'I think I will.'

He sat her on the stool facing the door. 'Would
you like the door shut?'

'No, I want an avenue of escape if I'm attacked by
a centaur.'

He looked at her sideways because that's where she
was. He went back to the coop he was repairing and
strangled a chicken for dinner.

She sat with her back and her head to the wall and closed her eyes – she was so tired. She went into a deep sleep and fell off the stool. The man guarded the wood like a wild-cat against any threat of a centaur. He lifted her back on the stool. She closed her eyes and all her life went still within her, in a true quietness. If only the chickens would stop crapping and clucking.

He had never in all his life felt at one with other people. The war had made it worse, people had tried to shoot him. His nature was passionate and inflammable, sometimes his balls caught fire. He was born solitary, but then everybody is born solitary. The sex desire was strong in him. Every morning he had a hard-on and had to wait half an hour until it went down before he could start work. He wanted to be left alone, only that, but you couldn't do it on your own. And now comes this woman seeking him. Already he could feel the stirring in his bowels. The porridge was on the move again. And the fusing of his knees. There was a searing sound and his knees fused together, his legs could only walk from the knees down. He glanced at her, poor thing, there was a touch of death in her face. Should he bury her? Was she waiting for him? If it was a fuck, yes.

The sense that all is well when it's true sex flooded him now and went down his trouser leg. He dreaded more than ever exposing himself. False things, what was he talking about? About twelve words a minute. He hadn't got a false thing. Let her go to her own class. What was she after? She was after a fuck. He couldn't turn her out. She was 'milady'. He was only a servant. They could turn him off. Lots of people turned him off, like Isadora Duncan, Florrie Ford and Lady Astor. He found himself gazing with hate at Constance as she sat in the hut.

She opened her eyes and he was there, so was she. He was looking at her asleep with hate. While she was asleep, had she done something to offend him? She was about to go. He was bending over his work with hate. He was making another clockwork tortoise with revolving eyes. She went across to him. She glanced at him, her face was stiff and tired.

'Good heavens, your face is stiff and tired,' he said.

Constance was late for tea. She found Mrs Bolton under the great beech tree on the knoll in front of the house with a telescope, looking for her.

'I wanted to see if you were coming, my lady. Sir Clifford was asking for his tea and I didn't want to make the tea.'

'Nonsense. Tea tastes the same no matter who makes it.'

She went in with a few wild-flowers in her hand.

'Sorry I'm late, Clifford. Why didn't you tell Mrs Bolton to make the tea?'

'I never thought of it,' he said ironically. 'Wouldn't you have been surprised if you had come in and found Mrs Bolton behind the tea pot?'

'Everyone's got to sit somewhere, so why not behind a tea pot?'

'What did you do?'

'I walked across the wood.'

She laid her gloves and flowers on the small tea table. They always took tea in Clifford's study. She was pouring the boiling water from the silver kettle into the silver tea pot. She found a little glass bowl for her flowers, arranging them lightly. The few daffodils and primroses, the odd violets and drooping wild-flowers, and two bits of pussy-willow.

'They'll all come up again,' he said and she put them down on the tea table and sure enough they came up again.

'What did you want a key to the hut for?'

'To open it, you fool. What did you think? The keeper was looking after the pheasants. Do you have to shoot them?'

'Yes. It's the only way to stop them. He feels the hut is his private lair, where he sleeps sometimes and keeps watch.'

'How in God's name can he sleep and keep watch at the same time? But is it *his* hut?'

He smiled at her with fine malice. It was one of the finest malices she had ever seen.

'Why not tell him that you have given me permission to use the hut.'

'I'm afraid he wouldn't hear me from here.'

The next afternoon Clifford and Constance went into the woods. The smoke partially obscured her from the chair. There was a faint scent of apple blossom and diesel in the air. She gathered a few apple blossoms and gave them to Clifford. He took them and looked at them and ate them. He felt the situation demanded it.

'"Thou still unravished bride of quietness,"' he quoted. 'Spring flowers always seem like that to me, much more than Greek vases.'

· 'Ah, but you can't smell a Greek vase,' said Constance.

She said she felt tired. She felt the situation demanded it. That evening with Clifford seemed interminable. She went to bed at nine o'clock and he carried on being interminable on his own.

Constance went out. She walked slowly, dimly, heeding nothing. She walked into trees. The hut was closed and locked. Yes, it was one of the silent, healing, unravished places. It was a pity about the chicken shit.

She stayed on and did not rise to her feet until the brown wet dog ran towards her, waving the wet feathers of her tail, and bit her ankle. The keeper followed, in a short oilskin coat and a big hat down over his eyes, he had to hold his head back at an angle to see ahead.

The keeper saluted very hastily, and in doing so he stuck his finger into his eye, his face red and hot with rain.

'I am just going,' she said, and went.

Chapter VII

SHE DISLIKED so intensely any sort of unconscious sexuality. It was very hard to have sex when you are unconscious. Better to avoid all sex than start messing about in ugly self-seeking, being screwed on a blanket in a chicken shed wasn't ladylike.

Was that what she wanted? Answer: Yes. And women, she knew, were worse at the game than men. Take Olive for instance. She picked up a man for the sole and simple purpose of putting herself over him. She would screw in a coal shed for a free hundred-weight of coal and come up black as a miner. So was it so bad if she was fucked in a chicken house? When women were into each other like Virginia Woolf and Vita Sackville-West, all women wanted to do was impose their own will and ego over the man. Mind you, with women between fifty and sixty the men charged.

Our civilization has one horrible cancer, one fatal disease: the disease of acquisitiveness. Many doctors have told their patients: 'I'm sorry to tell you but you

are suffering from a surfeit of acquisitiveness.' Neu-
rotics are people who climb trees, take all their
clothes off and sing 'Ave Maria'. There is no future
in climbing trees, stripping off and singing 'Ave
Maria'.

By now Mrs Bolton did everything for Clifford.
She drank his tea for him, ate his dinner for him, and
went to the loo for him. Constance saw them both
rise in their own conceit.

Dave Alsop also came to see Clifford. He was a
journalist on the *Tevershall & Stacks Gate News*. The
best thing that was ever in it was fish and chips.

There was dissent in the village after Princess Mary
had been given gifts from the miners and for her
wedding she was given exquisite gifts beyond anything the miners could afford. They were seeing
women slaving their insides out and it must have been
a ghastly sight, women with their insides out.

Clifford had a new vision of his own village. He
tended to think of it as unchanged. He knew in his
bones, yes in his bones, that it was unchangeable.
There was hostility by the miners to himself, and
Wragby, to the Chatterley vice-chairman, to all colliery owners, all managers, senior manager, chairman
and so on up to the Pope. They hated the manager,
the owner, the Archbishop of York, Bishop of
Durham, Cardinal Wolseley and Cardinal John.

He suddenly wanted to go down in the mines. The
colliers were hostile, were they? Then he would face
them and a lot of bloody good it did.

Colliers were waiting to see Wragby wiped out.

Well, he would show them. He went down the pit and sat eight hours in his chair 'showing them'. Unfortunately after four hours the miners had to go home and he spent the night in darkness, waiting for them to come back next morning. He came home that night covered in coal dust, he showed them, he showed them, he said through gritted teeth.

She felt she would surely die, in the interim. Her soul would have to have some relief, some hope, some touch. It was what she wanted. Not any revelation nor any new idea. Just a touch, even a good grope.

He was there, building a straw house, on four posts, for the birds.

'How nice, a little hut for the birds!' he said.

'A bit of shelter, like!' On which bit was it?

They both stood silent. She was aware of his deep, quiet breathing, except from his nose, one nostril had a whistle in it.

'It's spring!' she said. 'Oh joy! Have the birds made their nest? Please say yes, please say yes.'

'Ay! There's a jinny-wren's just theer!'

'Where? Where? Oh show me do!' and twirled.

He took her across to a tree where a wren had inserted his nest in a cunning fork of the bough. There was a little ball of moss, and grey hair and down.

'Oh, it was a little round ball of moss and grey hair and down.'

'Aye, there is a bloke in the village bald and they had every hair of his head to make this nest.'

'I wish I were a bird!' she said with infinite wistfulness.

'I think of you as a bird,' he said with a vulgar laugh.

He went back to his work making a clockwork tortoise with revolving eyes.

'You won't see me much longer,' she said.

'You're long enough,' he said.

'I've got you that key you wanted,' he said suddenly, in a lowered, altered voice.

'Did you?' she said in a higher altered voice.

He was in his shirt-sleeves, she was in a floral cotton dress. After a moment he came back with the key.

'Thank you so much. You're sure you won't mind if I come?' she said. 'Do say you won't.'

'You won't,' he said.

He looked away in the woods, all he saw were trees.

'If your ladyship doesn't mind me, I — you're very welcome to — I mean — you do as you please, it's your own place.'

She was silent for a moment, about three seconds.

'I don't want to interfere with you — or seem to.'

'You don't interfere with me, your ladyship.'

'Very well then,' she said softly. They'd had this conversation before.

He stood for some moments motionless, staring away into the wood. The trees were still there. Then automatically he reached for some straw from the heap. He was an automatic gamekeeper.

'It's the end of the day,' she said unthinking. Even then she got it right.

'Ay! Another!' he replied.

And his 'another!' rang strangely in her soul. God she was daft.

'Good-night, then!' she said.

And as she went home she saw a new moon, bright as a splinter of crystal in the western sky. It was so beautiful she started to cry. She came home with the front of her dress soaked.

Every day after this she went to the hut. Across there was a carpenter's bench, across there some tools on the bench, across there was some straw, across there a couple of bags of corn for the pheasants, across there a couple of old blankets. There was nothing else across there, that was it. On closer inspection there was a clockwork tortoise with revolving eyes.

He had only four hens. Constance would offer them a bit of corn in her hand, but the fierce mothers would peck savagely until they pecked her hand like it was a dart board. In the end she had to wear a boxing glove so when they pecked her she punched them.

Sometimes Soames would absentmindedly throw her a handful of corn. Whenever she went, she found him there. And she could tell, by the quick, eager way he looked round, that he was looking for her.

They seemed to be drawing together but they never touched. There was always a two-foot space between them. He carried a ruler to make sure the measurement stayed. When she saw him coming, a queer fire would melt her limbs and trickle down her body. She would wait and wait and wait. It was a foregone conclusion that he would screw her.

He always looked for her to be there and when she wasn't he would stop looking. He wanted her to be there; he even marked the place on the ground with a cross. He was streaming towards her from his knees, he was streaming towards her from the middle of his breast, from his teeth, from his nose, and other bits were all streaming towards her. To help keep up streaming towards her he drank half a bottle of malt whisky and even the whisky went on streaming towards her.

Gradually a sort of sleep or hypnosis was coming over him. He was losing his sense of time. He had to ask a policeman what time it was. He was melting away into the unknown but infinitely desirable flood of wholeness. What could a man do! Screw her.

The young pheasants began to hatch out, ready for Clifford to blast them from the skies. Constance came and wept with excitement and for the first time in her life she loved an old hen, the bright, fierce warm creature, with the chicks under her feathers so softly.

For two days Constance did not go into the wood, a tree fell on her. One of Clifford's aunts descended on them. She parachuted in. But she slipped away, breathless and bewildered.

There he was in his shirt-sleeves and she was in a knitted two-piece. She went straight towards him and she measured two feet between them.

'How many more are hatched?' she said.

'Oh, they're nearly all out,' he replied.

She quivered, he stood so near to her. Then she crouched down before the coop he had not shut up.

Tiny heads were poking out inquisitively between the yellow foliage of the old hen's feathers. He stood above her and she could see right up his nose.

He crouched down at her side and slowly he put his hand into the coop and brought forth a faintly piping chick. He put it in her hand.

'Isn't it adorable!' she cried.

In spite of herself, tears came into her eyes.

'It's one o' th' lively ones!' he said.

She bent her head, shook the tears from her eyes, the chick was beginning to devour, and looked up at him with a wet face.

'It's' — she said with a broken laugh — 'It's that they're so unafraid — ' and following the laugh came a torrent of tears.

He had to take the chick from her to stop it from being drowned. He laid his hand softly on her back and on her loins in a blind caress — dirty little devil. Her loins were at the back. He quickly put his hand to hers, and taking the little, piping bird, ushered it gently back.

His hand spread slowly round her body touching her breasts that hung inside her dress — dirty little devil.

'Shall yer come?' he asked.

She clung to his warm, relaxed, uncertain hand, the last uncertain hand he'd had was a 'Pontoon' in the war.

He drew her to him and she hid her face against him, which was what she wanted because he was an ugly bugger. It was too late now – it's started.

'Come to th' hut,' he said in a low voice.

'Oh no,' she said.

'Oh yes,' he replied.

She turned submissively, he stooped and shut the coop, swept up the chicken shit, and followed her. Romance was in the air. In the hut she sat down weakly on the stool. Again she could see right up his nose. He followed her and closed the door so that it was almost dark. Then he turned to her, feeling for her body.

'Oh no,' she said.

He felt with blind, overwhelming instinct the slope of her loins which were on the back and she submitted in a kind of sleep. He had to wake her up to keep her going. The groping softly, helplessly desirous caress of his hand on her body made her pass into a second consciousness, like sleep.

'Here, wake up,' he said. 'Otherwise you won't know it's t'appened.'

He held her with one hand and with the other threw down an old army blanket from the shelf.

'You can lie your head on the blanket,' he said.

One of the chickens had laid an egg and was clucking. Romance was in the air.

Obediently she lay with her head on the old army blanket. She felt him slowly, softly, gently but with queer blind clumsiness fumbling at her clothes.

'Oh no,' she said, the quiver of rapture like a flame

as he touched the soft naked in–slope of her thighs.
'Oh no, no, no,' she said.

The dog had started to circle them, barking at
them. Again he touched the soft slope of her thighs. It
was so long since she had done it, her fanny was dead.
The dog went on barking. She was not aware of the
infinite peace of the entry of his body into hers; that
was for the man. Little did she know it was also for
her. She was still in a kind of sleep.

'Oh no,' she moaned while he backed away, the
sweat pouring off him, the activity and the orgasm
was his. That's it, blame the poor bugger for doing it.

It was quite dark when he stopped. 'Oh,' she
moaned and he started banging away again.

Finally, when it was dark, he stopped and tried to
help her adjust her clothing. And when he opened the
door of the hut they saw through the oak-trees the
thin moon shining with extraordinary brilliance
through the holes in his underpants.

'Ah well!' he said to himself. 'It had to come.'

And he turned sharply, looking at her in surprise.
Then he touched her face with his fingers accidentally
poking her in the eye.

'I shall have to hurry home,' she said, half-blinded,
groping inside the hut. She was looking at him and
wanting him to kiss her as she stumbled half-blind
around the hut.

'Say something to me,' she said.

'I think we're going to get some rain tonight,' he
said.

'You aren't sorry, are you?'

'Me! No! It were a good t'fuck.'

There was a queer fluctuation in him. He said, 'Goodness me.'

'You are having a queer fluctuation,' she said. 'I'm glad.'

But even her saying it seemed to put her apart from him. She walked home quietly, and glad. He was right, it had been a good fuck. He was not sure of her. What did she really want? She wanted a fuck. What was it that his own heart wanted of her? He, too, wanted a fuck. He tried to shake off the spell of her. He shook himself vigorously but the spell did not come off.

When she was gone and it was night he went round the woods. All was still. The moon had set. He rubbed himself to get an erection and hoped she would be back before it went dawn. It was a still, lovely spring night. Yet also, full of dread: that queer, ever-shifting dread of the Midlands. The terrible Sheffield making endless knives, forks and spoons hall-marked EPNS. Unless you had that on them you were nobody.

A curious dread possessed him, a sense of defenceless-ness, so he got out his rifle and went into the woods shouting 'Hands up!' to the trees. He turned home, to the darkness of the wood, shouting 'Hands up!' He was not safe and by taking the woman and going forth naked to her he had exposed himself. She had seen his willy on the full and crossed herself. 'Hands up!' he shouted.

Slowly, carefully, with a hermit's scrupulousness he

got his supper of smoked salmon, roast pheasant, salade niçoise, peaches and cream and Château Margaux. He got it all through the back door of Lord Chatterley's kitchen from a friendly cook.

She found the doors of the house all closed. This annoyed her. All her life she had been annoyed by having to ring the bell.

Mrs Bolton said, 'Sir Clifford has got Mr Linley in with him. Should I put dinner back a bit?' she said.

Put it back a month. By then he'll be gone. Mr Linley was the General Manager of the collieries, a thin, red-faced man who was covered in layers of coal dust. His wife was a blonde, overdressed woman out of the country vicarage, very obsequious and toadying. She wasn't there. As a guest Mr Linley had brought Clifford a hundredweight of best nuts. Linley stayed to dinner and Connie was the hostess.

With joy she was cherishing her memories in reserve. She had been fucked by the gamekeeper. The man loved her with his body — what else? That she knew, he had given her nine inches of it, that she knew. She wanted the experience again. She had felt nothing so extreme. It wasn't as though it had gone right home to her. Nine inches were not enough. You have to go to twelve or fifteen inches. He had a hard year ahead of him.

She went to the wood in the afternoon, the next day. She was not conscious of anything except her own waiting. She came to the clearing of the hut and did some own waiting there. He was not there, she did same more own waiting and got bloody fed up. She wanted someone with nine inches.

She had better go back to tea. Mrs Bolton had made crumpets, had she suspected something? Far better to go home and come back, after tea, for some more screwing. 'Oh what a tangled web we weave when first we practise to deceive.'

She hurried home. And as she went, a fine drizzle began to fall.

'Is it raining again?' said Clifford.

'Yes, a fine drizzle has begun to fall.'

'We might have a game of bezique after tea.'

She looked at him in her slow, inscrutable way.

'Why are you looking at me in that slow, inscrutable way?' he said.

'I thought the situation demanded it – I better rest before dinner.'

'If you rest until tomorrow morning you could avoid dinner completely.'

'Perhaps Mrs Bolton will arm wrestle with you.'

'She will if I ask her. But I shall probably listen in to 2LO on the wireless.'

When Constance heard the loud-speaker switched on, in a velveteen sort of voice, announcing a series of London street cries, 'Violets! Stop thief, help, murder!', she slipped out of the side door and hurried across the park for another nine inches.

How still the wood was! Of course it was still, trees don't move about!

Constance waited in the doorway of the hut until at last came the owner of the nine inches slowly, unwillingly towards her, glancing at her with a swift, unwilling glance.

'You're late,' she said softly.

'Late?' he said. 'Did we have an appointment?'

He looked away not saying anything but he melted.

'You're melting,' she said. 'Do you want to come into the hut before you disappear?' she said, starting to undress.

'Are you sorry about yesterday?'

'No,' he said. 'T'were a good fuck.'

'I'm so glad,' she said.

'Don't you feel as you've lowered yourself, with the likes of me?

'Well, we were on the floor, we couldn't go any lower. Why? Do you feel I have lowered myself?'

'Wi' one o' your husband's servants like,' he said.

'You are not a servant, you are the gamekeeper,' she replied.

'I canna call yer your ladyship an' then screw thee.'

'I don't want you to call me your ladyship.'

'Do yo' like me?' he said.

'Yes!' she said pathetically.

'So yo' love me pathetically. Ah!' he said. ''Appen tha' does, 'appen tha does! But 'ow do we stan', thee and me?'

'Speak English for Christ's sake, man,' she said.

He gazed at her with bright, concentrated eyes. They were so concentrated they almost met on the bridge of his nose. 'Tha'lt be sorry, tha'lt be sorry!' he reiterated.

'For Christ's sake speak English, man.'

He gazed down on her, with a queer baffled smile in his eyes.

'Why are you gazing down at me with a queer baffled smile in your eyes?'

'Well,' he said slowly. 'If tha doesna care – if tha wants it.'

'If you knew how much it meant to me,' she said.

'What way?' he said.

'Lying down,' she said, 'then turn me over and do it from the back, doggie fashion.'

Suddenly his eyes changed, seemed to grow large and dark and full of flashing, leaping light. The eyes leaped up and down in the darkness. There were times when his eyes actually left his head.

Suddenly his resistance left him and his eyes came back. He folded round her, he raised her with his body.

'Oh no, oh no,' she said. She wanted him to kiss her and to speak to her and he did.

'I see there's trouble with the Saar. The Germans might re-occupy it.' His hands wandered with the blind instinct down to her loins. She wanted that as well.

'Let's go inside,' he said.

'Oh no,' she said.

He closed the door on them and swept up the chicken shit. He put the blanket on the floor then turned again, dirty little devil, and put his arms around her. He held her close with one hand and felt her body with the other. She heard the intake of his breath as he touched her. Beneath her frail petticoat, she was naked.

'Arggh eh! Tha'rt lovely to touch!' he said in that oafish voice of his as his fingers caressed the delicate warm secret skin of her ladyship's waist and hips. She kept her waist and hips a secret from him.

He kneeled and rubbed his cheek against her thighs and belly, dirty little devil. And when he took her she cried, 'Oh no, oh no.' Dirty little devil! And she wondered a little over the sort of rapture it was to him. It made her feel beautiful and very glad to be desirable. 'Oh no, oh no,' she said. He didn't seem to and kept banging away. And for the first time in her life she felt the animate beauty of her own thighs and belly and hips. Under his touch she felt a sort of dawn come into her flesh. Would it light up? And yet she was still waiting, waiting for that nine inches, nine inches plus.

'I can't stay long,' she said gently. 'You came so late. It's twenty past nine.'

> The Honourable Ormesly Gore
> Said I think this fucking is a bore
> You are covered in sweat
> And you haven't come yet
> Look at the time half-past bloody four.

He held her closer and tried to cover her naked legs with his body, it was physically impossible.

'I shall have to go or they will wonder,' she said.

He gave a sudden deep sigh, like a child coming

awake. Then he raised himself, and kneeling, kissed her thighs again.

'Oh no, oh no,' she said.

'Ay!' he said. 'Time's too short this time. Tha mun ta'e a' thy clothes off one time — shall ter? — on'y it'll ha'e ter be warmer.'

'What in God's name was the man talking about,' she thought.

He drew down her skirts and stood up, buttoning his own clothing unconsciously. He put the buttons in the wrong buttonholes leaving his flies all scrounged up with his shirt sticking out. He took his gun, looked for his hat which had fallen off when he was fucking and then quietly called for the dog.

'Dick! Here boy! Dick!' The dog didn't come because his name was Flossie. He locked the door, calling the dog.

'Appen as yer'd come ter th' cottage one time,' he said. 'If yer could slive off for a night.' He seemed near yet his voice was far away, in fact he was the local amateur ventriloquist.

'I shall come tomorrow if I can,' she said moving away.

'Good night, your ladyship,' came his voice from the top of a tree as she plunged into the dark-grey obscurity and fell over.

Chapter VIII

THE NEXT DAY she felt she could not go to the hut to him. What kept her away? It was his garbled use of the English language to the point where you could not understand it. She winced when when she thought of him. 'Tha mun ta'e a' thy clothes off one time, s'all ter?' Surely it was not she he was speaking to?

That afternoon she could not keep still. She made a dozen plans (1) to climb the Eiger, (2) swim the Channel, (3) win at Wimbledon, and (4) take the gold medal in the 5,000-metre Olympics. She would not go to the wood. No, she would go to Marehay, through the little iron gate of the park, and round Marehay farm.

When she was out she felt better. She walked on stupefied, noticing nothing and fell into ponds. She came to Marehay farm, the dog attacked her, bellowing round her.

'Come, Bell, have you forgotten me?' she said.

Mrs Flint appeared. She was a woman of

Constance's own age, size, colour and had the same number of legs.

'Why Bell! Bell! Barking at Lady Chatterley! Bell! Be quiet!'

'He used to know me,' said Constance.

'Why of course he did. But it's so long since he's seen you. I hope you are well. Shall you come in and have a look at the baby. He's grown now, you'd hardly know him.'

As she went in to see the baby the dog attacked her.

'Bell, Bell, barking at Lady Chatterley. Bell, be quiet,' the woman commanded.

Constance played with the baby. She had given it a shawl when it was born, and a rattle for Christmas. Bell recommenced barking.

'Why Bell, Bell, barking at Lady Chatterley. Bell be quiet,' the woman commanded.

The two women enjoyed talking about the baby. The dog recommenced barking.

'Why Bell, Bell, barking at Lady Chatterley. Bell be quiet,' the woman commanded.

'My husband won't know what's become of me.'

'What does he expect you to be then?' Mrs Flint insisted. 'A barn gate?'

'Yes, he often wishes I was a barn gate.'

The last thing Lady Chatterley heard was the dog barking at her as she departed.

On the way back a man stopped in front of her. It was Soames. He was not wearing trousers. She gave a cry of fear and then he said, 'Urgghh! Are you coming to the hut?'

'No, I was going home.'

He looked down at her in a flare of anger because he wanted to. 'You wasn't sliving past and not meanin' to see me, was you?' he said putting his arm round her, determined.

'Not now!' she said, trying to push him away.

'But you said,' he replied rather angrily and his arms tightened instinctively, against his will, around her and his body pressed strangely upon her. She felt it sticking in her. Her instinct was to fight him. Why fight? Why fight anybody? Her will seemed to live here and she was limp. He held her in his arms, then he half carried her, the other half had to get there on its own. He took her to where there was a heap of dead boughs. He threw out one or two fir boughs and folded his coat. She stood by mute and helpless. Then he took her and laid her down.

'Oh no, oh no,' she said.

A strange thrilling sensation that she had never known before woke up where he was within her. In wild thrills like wild bells, ting-a-ling, ting-a-ling they went. And she clung to him uttering in complete unconsciousness strange, wild, inarticulate little cries like eeh, aah, ooh, oo oo, and it was too soon, it was only a quarter to ten.

Till he came into her again, and the thrills woke up once more, wilder and wilder, like bells ringing clang, clang, clangety clang, tinkle, tinkle, tinkle.

And he was still too, he was shagged out. It was a perfect stillness, he lay upon her and fell asleep and started to snore.

Oh, oh, romance was in the air. Good God, he had woken up and started to do it again.

'We came off together this time,' said the oaf.

'Jolly good,' she replied. Like all upper-class ladies, she had not noticed. Rising from the forest floor she brushed off the ants, slugs and snails. He dusted the fir needles from her dress and took them quietly from her hair. All the while he listened intently for the motorized wheelchair of Lord Chatterley and his double-barrelled shotgun. He knew him to be a dead shot and he did not want it to be him.

She thought of the man in the wood and she was grateful to him for his service which was better than her own garage. She was like a volcano – at moments she surged with desire and passion like a steady stream of white hot lava with puffs of sulphurous smoke issuing from her knickers. Clifford thought she had stomach trouble. In some mysterious way she felt his domination over her and against the very love inside her. She revolted like one of the Bacchae, madly calling on Iacchos, the bright phallus that had no independent personality behind it. He was but a temple servant, the guardian and keeper of the bright phallus which was hers, her own. A mile away in his cottage Soames did not know she was claiming owner-ship of his prick.

She could feel her body, like the dark interlacing of the boughs of the oak-wood, humming inaudibly with myriad, unfolding buds. Meanwhile the birds of desire had their heads on their shoulders, asleep with delight, in the vast interlaced intricacy of her body. Go girl go!

She thought of his beautiful silky skin, his mouth, it was rather angry and smelled of tobacco and Brown Windsor. And not his figure! He should be taller, more graceful. She avoided looking at him naked – it put her off. Oh those huge feet. He was a good fuck and that is all she wanted.

How Clifford had changed from the once pale, poem-writing idealist Clifford! 'After all,' he said, 'you've got all the important feelings there in Racine.'

'Yes,' she said, 'I'm sure that is true.'

'Of course it's bloody true, that's why I said it.'

Mrs Bolton brought in the tray with a cup of some nourishing hot drink which she had introduced as a nightcap for him. It was Horlicks laced with brandy and a wad of chloroform.

'Good-night Clifford! Do sleep well!'

'Good-night.' He watched her with lynx eyes, his own were at the opticians. Even that she could forget! And he was too proud, too offended to remind her of the kiss though it was but a formality. So she gave him a formality.

She drifted out with her glass of Horlicks, closed the door behind her. He gazed angrily at the door-panels, it was pointless gazing angrily at door-panels. Mrs Bolton had put him in the day-time on Kepplers Malt. He knew he was crippled, he stared angrily at the door-panels.

His dread was the night when he couldn't sleep with anybody. But Mrs Bolton had added half a bottle of brandy to the Horlicks until it had turned brown. It seemed to help him into the land of dreams.

Mrs Bolton would spent the night wondering who Lady Chatterley's lover was. It was impossible, there was no man at Marehay and she couldn't do it with nobody. There was Soames in the woods. Mrs Bolton knew that when young many times he had had his hands in her knickers. Then Lady Chatterley would never stoop to him. He was so common and that wife of his had made him commoner. He might be attractive to a low sort of woman, like a dwarf, but for a refined woman, he was a snarling nasty brute.

Still, you never know. When women did fall, they sometimes fell in love with creepie-crawlers. So her ladyship might enjoy demeaning herself. But there, she'd had her own way so long she might be asking to be bullied.

Mrs Bolton was thinking of Lady Chatterley's lover. There was Soames in the woods, of course, with his nine inches. He might be attracted to lower women like a dwarf but for the refined woman he was just a snarling nasty brute with the attraction of nine inches of gristle that hung down his trousers to his knee.

Constance was in bed. Soames, after she had left him, went to the hut, swept up the chicken shit, and put the blankets down in anticipation of her return. He even had his evening meal of pâté, smoked salmon, venison cutlets, New Jersey potatoes, asparagus and Crêpes Suzette with a bottle of Château Lafitte. This woman had disorientated him. He could no longer tell East from West. He did not really care. He wanted the woman. Nevertheless he made his rounds cautiously. He was like one in a dream. He kept walking over cliffs but he refused to be conscious of it as he lay half unconscious at the foot of a cliff.

He went at last to the hut and sat a while waiting for an erection. He looked out at the stars and the silent darkness of growing trees. And for some reason they were like the body of a woman. In his opinion some women had bodies like trees. He tried to screw a tree and all he got was a prick full of splinters.

After gazing a long time motionless into the night, becoming again conscious of a certain weariness that was upon him, he shut the door of the hut, he went heavily to sleep. Yet he woke, uneasily, after a while. It was still dark night. He put on his coat and his hat, took his gun, and went out, followed by the dog. He walked away into the wood, without knowing in which direction, if he had continued on this course, he would have reached Bexhill-on Sea and the Channel. Finally he reached Bexhill-on-Sea and he did not know what to do so he climbed uphill to the knoll, to listen and look out. He heard nothing, he saw nothing. So much for knoll-climbing. The world was utterly still, wan and dead. He moved to a fresh knoll, hearing nothing and seeing nothing. There must have been better knolls. He went back across the wood and when he got there there was nothing to do so he did that for half an hour. The chill that was in his heart, and the pain of uncertainty that was in his bowels must have been what he had for dinner or the half-bottle of Château Lafitte. He reached the gate to Wragby Manor, he opened that gate. That was one of the things you could do with a gate. He came to the top of a knoll and he slid backwards down it. The light was burning downstairs in Sir Clifford's room who was recovering from the Horlicks, brandy and chloroform.

Mrs Bolton woke up and watched the dim figure of the gamekeeper. She recognized him by his dog. He had such a plain face you could only recognize him by his dog. She would not go out. If she stayed in and he stayed out, the result would be a draw. Mrs Bolton was making up her mind to go out and to greet him when she saw him turn and disappear. Yes, he had gone and the proof was he wasn't there.

Chapter IX

CONSTANCE WAS sorting out a lumber room on the top floor. She was sorting out the store room. And among the things, carefully wrapped up to preserve it from wild animals like wolves and bears, there was a charming cradle. It had such touching proportions so she touched them. It was a cot, a 100-year-old cot. She was moved. Mrs Bolton just picked her up and moved her somewhere else.

'It seems a pity there isn't a little baby to put in it now,' said Mrs Bolton.

'Yes!' said Constance vaguely. 'I suppose it is.' She hesitated, before she added: 'But there may be, you know.'

'Oh, your ladyship, that would be good news! — But you're not expecting it, are you?'

She had a few friends in to tea. 'Could you believe Lady Chatterley still has hopes of a son and heir?'

'Never!' cried the women. 'Why, it's impossible with his willy!'

'No, Sir Clifford's legs are paralysed, but – ' and a series of suggestive nods. 'And you know he's so much better! And you can see his strong arms, shoulders and chest. He's got a splendid chest.'

'Wonders'll never cease! It seems you can all but kill a man, but he'll be able to do something that way with a woman.'

Mr Winter called one afternoon. He was a well-bred man of sixty-five with appalling halitosis. Clifford spoke to him from a distance. He had a very keen interest in and talked about coal. They agreed you found it in the ground, you dug it out and then sold it.

'Oh no, coal isn't what it used to be!'

'Oh,' said Sir Clifford, 'then what's it supposed to be?'

Mr Winter didn't answer.

'I hear you might be having a baby,' said Mr Winter.

There was a silence, Clifford was startled, frightened, infuriated, bewildered, and a little flattered, in that order.

'Well Sir!' he said, backing away from his breath. 'Of course nothing is certain. But we can hope!'

'Oh, but there is hope?' said Winter taking a glance at Clifford's bottom half. Was there any hope in his trousers?

This man had been a friend of King Edward and was almost willing to die for the King. So far he hadn't done so, why should he?

One morning Constance was arranging the flowers in the room.

'I say, Connie, have you heard the rumour? You're going to provide Wragby with an heir.'

She did not start, she had a flat battery. Then she said, 'Why, where have you heard such a rumour?'

'From Mr Winter.'

'And what did you say?' she asked.

'I said, well, because he had bad breath I asked him to keep his distance.'

She pondered for a while, for about half an hour, quite a long ponder. 'What did you say to Mr Winter?'

'I said you have got bad breath and I said Constance may be going to have a child.'

'But,' she said, 'if I may be going to have a child, what would you feel?'

'I would feel your stomach,' said Clifford.

Still she thought of Soames. He was passionate with an underground passion. He preferred to screw down the coal-mine. She didn't want to be committed to him but she wanted to go to him. (Make up your bloody mind, woman!) At the thought of him a flame went through her bowels. She wanted his children, unfortunately he didn't have any.

But he had not touched her heart. Soames held her with passion and an occasional brace of grouse but nothing and nobody held her altogether. If it wasn't for her stays she'd have fallen apart.

She was thinking of Soames whom she had not seen for some time. She found a tenderness for him spring up in her again – doinggg! To see him she had to go outside her own sphere. It was an excursion just

like a cheap day-return to Herne Bay and the desire
for an excursion was coming over her again. She was
on the verge of booking a cheap day-return trip to
Herne Bay.

And when the coal was gone would they too
disappear off the face of the earth? No, they would
make their way back to Africa where there were
elephants. So there was hope.

She told Clifford she had had tea in Uthwaite in
Miss Bentley's tea shop. 'So you had tea at Miss
Bentley's tea shop. Oh yes, you have to be in a tea
shop if you want tea.'

Miss Bentley was a sallow old maid, dark skinned
with a rather large nose which obscured her vision.
She served teas with careful intensity as if she was
administering an oft-repeated sacrament. She could
only see you if you stood to one side. Yet she lived
dangerously. She didn't wear any knickers.

'It must be splendid', said Clifford, 'to put so much
effort into making tea.'

'Oh yes!' Constance imitated Miss Bentley's hushed
murmur.

'Look, I can't hear you in a hushed murmur,' said
Clifford. 'And I suppose you said I was blooming?'

'Yes, I said you were wonderfully well.'

'Do you think she has a special feeling about me?'

'Yes, you are her *roman de la rose*.'

'Come, Constance, don't be too far-fetched.'

So Constance stopped being too far-fetched.

'We are a queer couple, you and I, Connie. In a
sense, we belong to one another. The house belongs

to the Bradford & Bingley and we belong to each
other.'

'Yes, I think so,' she said.

'There is something eternal between us, don't you
think?'

That frightened her a little. The only thing that was
eternal between them was breakfast, so that was two
fried eggs and bacon. Yes, that was what was eternal
between them, breakfast.

'There is a certain conjunction between our mortal
selves,' he went on.

Wouldn't it be wonderful if he had a stroke? It
would be a stroke of luck for her.

'I think we are eternal,' said Clifford.

'Yes, two eggs and bacon,' she stressed.

'For God's sake, be careful what sort of man you let
be the father of your child. He mustn't be of the
lower orders.'

'But there is no child,' she said.

Chapter X

COMING DOWNSTAIRS in the morning she found Soames's dog Flossie running around the hall making faint whimpers and piddling down the table leg.

'Hullo, Flossie!' said Constance. 'What are you doing here?' And what she was doing there was piddling down the table leg.

The dog ran towards the door of Clifford's room. Why was the voice of Soames speaking to Clifford? Then she said to the dog:

'You want your master? Come along then!'

The dog slid in and widdled on Lord Chatterley's wheelchair.

'I had to let Flossie in,' she said. 'She was flooding the house.'

Gently Soames kicked its arse. 'I'll push her out,' he said to Lord Chatterley and he avoided looking at Constance for fear of an erection.

'I found her in the hall,' said Constance.

Once she was physically near him Constance was

only aware of him and Clifford was a mere cypher and there was fire in her nethers. Should she call the fire brigade?

Something in her rejoiced but she wanted to know what his business was.

'Did I interrupt you?' said the silly girl. Of course she had interrupted them.

'No, no,' said Sir Clifford, trying to be tolerant.

She looked at Soames. He had on his furtive, game-keeper's look, which she did not like. Yet his physical presence fascinated her. Oh the burning in her nethers.

'These poachers got three rabbits apiece on 'em an' two of 'em wa' does as would ha' case in a day or two.'

She was rather piqued that her presence had no visible effect on him at all, there was no swelling in his trousers.

'How are the little pheasants?' she asked him.

'Still little,' he said.

'I shall come and see them soon,' she said.

'Oh Christ,' he thought. 'You'll find them running around nice and independent. Soon they be ready for Sir Clifford to shoot them,' he said.

Not even the judge of judges would have suspected that she had allowed him to make free with her body. She did not charge him. He was just one lucky gamekeeper being able to screw the ladyship of an aristocrat free of charge on an army blanket.

She went that evening to the hut, and found him there, apparently waiting for her.

'You see I've come,' she said.

He smiled. 'I can see that,' he said. 'I'm not daft.'

He was in his shirt-sleeves working at something. He was making a clockwork tortoise with revolving eyes. He wore his flannelette shirt with bone buttons on the wrist. Yet his wrists looked so full of life. Yes folks, wrists full of life and under his clothing did he have that beautiful white body that she had seen? Yes, yes, yes yes! Steadily growing the flame of passion went over her and down her knickers and up her back again. Suddenly she said:

'I have told Sir Clifford I might have a child.'

He stopped in his tracks. His bottle went.

'You told him that?' he said, his legs shaking. Sir Clifford was a dead shot.

'Yes, you see, I might.'

'You don't do nothing to stop it, then?' he said, his bottle going again a second time.

He put his hat on again, it still fitted.

'And Sir Clifford would take it for his own, would he?' he said.

'Oh no!' she said.

'So there was no mention of me being the father?'

He breathed a sigh of relief and came out from behind a tree.

'I'm going abroad with my father next month. He could think I have found somebody else.'

'How long will you be abroad?'

About five foot six inches.

'How long? Until the middle of June.'

He gazed at her. So he was going to lose her for a

time. He thought very fast. Perhaps he could fuck
Mrs Bolton. At last he turned to her with a quick,
awkward movement and fell over.

'Was that what you wanted me for, a baby?' he
said. 'You didn't think much of me, like?' he said.

She looked up at him dumbly.

'I liked your body,' she said dumbly.

'Then we're quits! I like yours!' he said.

As long as they could go on screwing everything
was okay. Wrong! He looked at her a little mockingly.
He knew she wanted to keep relatively free of him.
Wrong! She wanted to keep as much of him as she
could.

'And do you like it when I feel of you?' he said.

'Yes, I love it,' she admitted.

What a couple of dummies; as long as they could go
on screwing, the child could be ignored.

'Eh well then – Have you left your underthings off
for me?'

'Yes!'

His eyes were flashing, on-off-on-off.

'Let's go inside then, and be private.'

He closed the door of the hut. This started the hens
clucking. He pulled off his boots and leggings and
trousers and stood in his shirt, the tip of his willy
showing below the hem of his shirt. What a bloody
fool he looked!

'Now you can feel me if you've a mind to,' he said
coming to her and lifting back her skirts and,
coming to her naked body with a queer, constrained
smile of passion. And she put her arms around him

under his shirt and she met pimples. She was afraid of his body. She shrank afraid, away. Difficult to do when you've somebody thirteen stones on top of you.

And when he said, in the queer heart-sad croon of the voice of his passion: 'Tha'rt nice; tha'rt nice!' her body loved it. But something in her spirit, and in her will, stiffened with resistance, from the intimacy, and from the peculiar haste of his possession. And if the sharp ecstasy of her own passion did not overcome her, if her spirit managed to keep aloof, then his buttocks butting away would seem ridiculous to her, and the sort of anxiety of his penis to come to its conclusion would seem almost farcical. And then it would occur to her that this was love, this ridiculous butting of buttocks, and wilting of a poor little penis. And she would say to herself, as so many men, poets and all, have said, that surely the God that created man, created him a reasoning being, and yet forced to procreate himself in this humiliating ridiculous posture, all buttocks and bollocks, created him surely out of savage irony and contempt for his own creation.

'Tha mun com' ter th' cottage for a naight, sholl ter?' he said to her, his speech getting broader. 'Tha mun com an' slaip wi'me, afore tha goos wi' thy feyther. Shall ter? When sholl ter? We can be long at it.'

What was the oaf trying to say?

He seemed to slide through centuries, thousands of years of human culture, in this hour with her. When she came, he was an ordinary man, not very different from Tommy Dukes or Clifford. But when his eyes began to dilate and flash, he began to slide back through the centuries.

Now in another breath he had moved forwards again another thousand years.

'Shall yer come one night ter th' cottage?' he said, quite changed and distant, in an almost ordinary voice. And now, instead of naight, sharp, it was ni–ight, with a long heavy i – it seemed to weigh him down. And now also he did not urge further. He left her to it. And now she had to say yes to him for fear he should not ask her again. She wanted to go to the cottage but he made her admit it.

'Yes! Shall I! Do you think I dare?' she said.

'Yes, we can be at it longer,' he said. And back he went the thousand years again, but warmer, more assured. When he returned from his thousand years, it was raining.

'When sholl ter come?' he said.

'Sunday?' she said faintly.

He quickly opened the door of the hut.

'Should I dust thee?' he said.

And he gently dusted her down, his hand passing softly over the curves of her body, up her skirt and down her knickers.

'Tha'rt good cunt, aren't ta?' he said softly.

'What's that?' she said. 'What is cunt?'

'It's what a man gets when 'e's inside thee! – Yo' wouldn't know what *cunt* is, though,' he added, a little mocking, taking a great stride suddenly and landing back in the twentieth century where he was currently living.

He was cold again. She didn't know it but people thought *he* was a cunt. Only when he was leaving her he said:

‘ ‘Sunday then! What time?’

‘Why – sometime after ten.’

‘All right! An’ I s’ll wait for yer here, at this gate. – If anything stops you though – ?’

‘If I don’t come,’ she said, ‘you walk towards the house, and see if there’s a light in my bedroom. If there’s a light in my bedroom, after ten o’clock, it means I can’t come. – So you walk home again.’

‘All right. I know which is your bedroom. It’ll be the one with the light on.’

God he was dim.

The world seemed like a dream. The trees seemed to be bulging and surging at anchor on the tide. What in God’s name trees were doing surging at anchor on the tide is anybody’s guess. She herself was a different creature, sensitive and alert, quietly slipping among the living presence of having trees at anchor on the tide.

It was new and wonderful, but she was still uneasy. She knew she had got it from him. It was nothing that penicillin couldn’t cure. She had really touched him at last. He looked touched. The stars opened like eyes, with a consciousness in them, and the sky was filled with a soft, yearning stress of consolation, mostly over Manchester. Everything had its own anima. Elephants had their own anima.

The quick of the universe is in our bodies, deep in us, somewhere around the ankles. As we see the universe, so it is, but also it is much more than we ever see or can see (Eh?). And the soul changes in us, it turns over. That is face down with a new creative move, the whole aspect of all things change and we see the universe as it is with trees at anchor with the tide.

Connie felt this change happen to herself. The man had caused her soul to turn so it was facing the other way. She felt frightened and shrinking. She was down to five foot three inches. She had got a new nakedness.

She now believed she would have a child. For some reason she felt drawn to Mrs Bolton, as if they had something in common – Clifford's legs.

The two women were working together in the garden.

'Is it many years since you lost your husband,' she said softly to Mrs Bolton.

'Twenty-three,' said Mrs Bolton.

'Have you tried looking for him?' she said.

'It's funny. One day he booked a cheap day-return to Herne Bay and never came back. He just disappeared somewhere in Herne Bay.'

Mrs Bolton's eyes suddenly filled with tears. Constance put a bucket under her.

In the afternoon, she felt she must speak to Soames. So for Clifford she did one last nude Charleston.

She walked on slowly, hoping to find him and his smooth white body in the cottage where he rarely was. The double daffodils stood in tubs near the door and the red double tulips were all out. The door was open and there he was sitting at the table in his shirt-sleeves eating.

'May I come in?' she said, as he rose and came to the door.

'Come in,' he said.

The sun shone into the room which smelled of lamb chops and salmon steak on the grid-iron. The black potato-saucepan was on a piece of paper by the white hearth, the fire was red, rather low, the bar dropped, the kettle singing.

He had his plate with potatoes and the remains of the chop[1] on the table that was covered with a dark chocolate oil-cloth. Why he should want to cover the remains of the chop with a dark chocolate oil-cloth is a mystery.

'Champagne?' he said, setting a glass in front of her.

'You are very late,' she said. 'Do finish eating.'

'I'm trying to finish eating,' he said.

He began to finish eating again rather hurriedly and unwillingly. She had never seen a man so unwilling to eat.

'Shall I take your plate away?' she said.

'Yes. Don't take it too far, I need it for breakfast.'

And she tramped across the uneven brick floor to the dark scullery at the back.

'There's no light in here,' she said.

---

[1] Lord Chatterley's kitchen had difficulty getting him his usual supplies.

'No, it's in here.'

'Will you have a cup of tea too?' she asked him.

'Don't mind if I do,' he said, putting pâté de foie gras on a Bath Oliver and washing it down with Moët & Chandon.

A quick laugh went over his face, round his ears, over his eyebrows, across his forehead and down again.

'I thought,' he added, 'what if anybody did happen to come and see you, supposing it was Sir Clifford with his gun?'

'It wouldn't matter, he would just shoot you. He wouldn't think anything,' she said.

'Everyone's got to think of something. You're think ing of being my wife, I was thinking of Julius Caesar.'

'Oh good. He's quite harmless now, he's dead.'

'Ay, I was thinking of him when he was dead, just to be on the safe side. An' you like it, you say, to be my wife sometimes?'

'Yes!' she said. 'When we're doing it, that's when.'

'It suits me down to the ground (he couldn't go lower) – as long as it lasts,' he added.

She reproached him. Last time it had lasted eighteen minutes, she had checked it with her watch.

He drank his tea with his hands in his pockets which made it very difficult to lift up the cup. Suddenly he lifted his head, and pressed back his shoulders, stretching his body in the quiver of desire, he lowered his trousers.

'Shall we go upstairs?' he asked softly.

'No! Not today, not today!' she cried and hid under the table.

Looking underneath he looked searchingly upsidedown in her eyes, looking for the latent desire in her. He pulled up his trousers but did not button them in case she changed her mind.

She emerged from under the table.

'Will you have some more tea?' she asked him.

At last he drank, the tea wetting his brown moustache and wiping it automatically on his fingers. What a boon to have automatic fingers!

'Do you like having a moustache?' she asked him, trying to detract him from sexual activity. 'It hides your mouth – one can't see what sort of mouth you've got.'

With a queer face he took his moustache in both hands and lifted it aside, sticking his mouth out a little till it looked like a chicken's bum, as he did so showing a mouthful of awful dentistry. They appeared to be like tombstones in a deserted cemetery.

'Kiss me!' she whispered. 'Kiss me because you like me, not because you want me.'

It took a while for the oaf to work that out.

He lowered his moustache and trousers, pushed back his chair and opened his arms, with a little gesture half of command.

'Come then!' he said.

She went over to his arms, and he bent his head over her, kissing her tenderly, and with a sort of grief, and holding her fast to his breast.

'But you love me?' she asked.

'It looks like it,' he said. And he looked like it.

'And don't you care whether I love you or not?' she said.

'Nay!' he said with a faint smile. 'What's the good o' carin'?'

She did not understand him.

It was perfectly clear he had just said 'what's the good of caring' in a North Country accent.

'You an' me!' he said. 'It's not as if we could think o' marryin'.'

'Couldn't you think of it?' she asked, searching his face and finding his nose in the middle of it.

Back came his eyes to her. She now had two pairs.

'Why, could ya'?' he said.

Ya? Wasn't that German?

She thought about it in a wavering fashion. She wavered out the door into the garden, round the house, then wavered back again.

'I feel married to you,' she said.

'Well,' he said, 'wavering once around the house doesn't mean we're married.'

'But why shouldn't I be your wife sometimes, as long as we live? Why must it be a regular marriage?'

He pondered her words.

'And you think it could be like that?' he pondered. He went on pondering. 'Off and on while we live?'

'Why not?' she said, pushing back his moustache with her fingers, and kissing him on those hidden chicken bum lips and quivering at her own temerity.

'Why are you quivering at your own temerity?' he said.

'It's my own temerity,' she said.

'Why couldn't it? You wouldn't want me always in this cottage, always, always, always, till doomsday, would you?'

Oh no, he couldn't wait till doomsday, the lease runs out before that.

'It'd be nice if you could be my wife sometimes, while we live.' After that it would be very difficult.

She was sitting on his knee, and still stroking his moustache, and touching his lips, teasing him.

'Yes!' she said, clinging to him suddenly. 'Let us see! Let me be your wife off and on. When you're on I will be your wife and when you're off, that's it.'

'Yes!' he said in good English. 'I will! I will whenever we can. I would like to get on now.'

So saying he tried to get on her.

'We'll call one another by no names,' he said hastily.

'Perhaps not. But give me your hand. Hold my hand fast.'

He clasped her hand as fast as he could. He held her close, in silence, in the warm little room, with all the wild sunshine of spring outside. And clinging close like a child she went to sleep. And he, his head drooping above her, passed also into a doze, infinitely soothing and still. Twice she slipped to the floor with a thud and he had to pick her up. She lay heavy and still in his lap. God what excitement! He leaned his face against her hair with a deafening snore that rattled the knives and forks on the empty table.

'Shall we be going then?' he said finally.

'No,' she said.

'What will they be thinking back at the home?'

'I don't know,' she said. 'I'm not a mind-reader.'

He shut the door and locked it. Flossie the dog ran round in silent joy, lifting the feather of her tail and biting Lady Chatterley's leg.

'Heel, heel!' he said, kicking the dog's arse. 'Ay, but – ' he said no more. He could only manage so many words a day and he'd reached his limit.

'Now if you come to th' hut and I'm not there, an' you want to find me, what you want to do is find the hatchet an' chop a bit o' wood. I s'll hear you – an' Flossie will. Chop a bit o' wood on th' block, you know. We s'll hear that.'

'All right!' she said.

So to get a shag she had to chop some wood. Who said romance in England was dead?

'An' if I don't see you afore Sunday, I s'll be waiting for you at ten o'clock. An' if you don't come, I s'll walk up to th' house. That's right, isn't it? If there's a light in the room, you can't come.'

'That's right!' she assented. 'Then you bugger off.'

'Goodbye!' she said. She wished she was saying it for good. Heaven only knows why. She didn't know.

She went blindly towards the gate, and walked into it.

Clifford had come in his wheelchair to the top of the drive, he had come under a rookery and was covered in bird shit.

'It's so lovely, Clifford!' she said. 'I went to sleep.'

If you're going to tell lies, tell a big one!

'Where did you sleep?'

'In the keeper's hut, sitting in the sunshine. I went fast asleep.'

He was astounded. His wife had mastered the art of falling asleep upright on a stool.

'Why didn't you come and meet me?'

'Oh I should imagine you'd want something different from me than to come and meet you.'

'Oh Clifford, don't! It's so lovely.'

'Am I lovely?' he said desperately. 'The cuckoo only jeers at me, even the rooks shit on me. How dare I come and meet you, in a bath-chair covered in bird shit! Why doesn't somebody shoot me!'

'I don't know, Clifford. Why doesn't someone come and shoot you?'

'I was asking you,' he said.

Constance took charge of the wheelchair. Without his hands on it, he controlled it with great difficulty.

'You missed your tea,' he said. 'Don't you want to go in and have some with Mrs Bolton?'

With her steering they hit a tree and Clifford was catapulted from his wheelchair. With great difficulty they restored him to the chair. She looked at him startled, wondering what he saw. Basically he saw her.

'Was it horrid of me not to be home to tea?'

'My dear child, the only thing that is horrid is my existence, I ought to be shot, as a horse with broken legs is shot.'

'No, Clifford!' she said. 'I won't hear any of that!

You haven't broken legs. No, I won't let them shoot you till you have broken legs.'

She left him there in the chair on the drive, at the crest of the park slope, to get on with it.

Mrs Bolton was in the hall.

'How well you're looking, my lady!' said Mrs Bolton. 'You're a different woman.'

'No I'm not, I'm still the same woman. I went to sleep in the woods,' she said.

'Why?' said Mrs Bolton. 'Is your bed uncomfortable? Sir Clifford wouldn't mind a bit if you told him you would be out.'

'But how is one to know?' said Constance resentfully.

'Well, either you're going out or staying in, one of the two.'

'You mustn't mind, Constance, if I grouse a bit sometimes. The spring makes it gruesome for me,' said Clifford.

'Why don't you forget, forget yourself.'

Then he would have to think he was someone else who would do his worrying for him. He tried to think he was Bonar Law but it didn't help.

'I'm encumbered with my own deadness!' he said.

'Look, your top half is all right. Why not enjoy that?'

'Do you mean you love me as Héloïse loved Abélard, after he was castrated?' he said.

'I don't know!' she said. 'I'm not Héloïse. But Abélard never wished they had killed him. He was very much alive and active.'

'Ah, but he had his feet,' said Clifford.

He was quiet for a while – two days in fact.

'After all, you can hear the larks and feel the sun,' she said.

'Not at the same time,' he said.

'And you have the mine to be interested in and all the things you studied in Germany like pick-axes and shovels.'

'I'm so bored I could cry and howl.'

He was quiet for another two days.

'Why should you cry and howl, Clifford? You could attract wolves.'

Chapter XI

CLIFFORD WANTED to go into the wood. He had to be helped from one wheelchair to another. His arms and shoulders were strong and he was very clever in swinging himself from one place to another. He once did it from England to France.

She was choking as he puffed away all round the house, filling every room with diesel fumes.

He was in rather high feather this bright May morning. The larks were singing over the park as Clifford blazed away at the pigeons and crows.

'Listen,' he said. 'Wragby is the ship that sails on ahead in the voyage of discovery.'

'What has she discovered?' asked Constance.

'Who first emerged into the open waters of liberty: Wragby! You're quite right about it being beautiful,' Clifford said. 'It is amazingly beautiful. What is quite as lovely as an English spring!' as he blazed away at rabbits. The brow of the hill was sheer blue, and virgin – the only one in the district.

Clifford had kept the chair going till he got to the top of the slope, for fear of getting stuck. Constance followed slowly behind, to be alone. The oak-buds had opened soft little brown hands. Everything was so tender and full of life. Why oh why need man be so tough, always tough and insentient, hard as iron, gripping the wrong things, and missing everything. Why could human life never be soft and tenderly coming unfolded into leaf and blossom? If men were leaves of grass, why was it never tender young green grass, new and soft with spring? Even with the oaks, with all their craggy hardness, that fought so many winters, even they took off their myriad gloves. Why couldn't men be like that? What utter bollocks!

The chair began slowly to advance down the long slope, in the broad, noble riding, slowly sailing as down the slope of a wave. Clifford sat and steered, and when he had disappeared the keeper came striding with long strides down the hill. She heard his steps, and glanced round in fear. He gave a hasty half-salute.

'I heard the chair-motor,' he said, in a soft voice. 'Shall ye' come tonight?'

'Tonight?' she said, looking bewildered into his eyes.

'Ay! Come tonight!' His voice was low and infinitely caressive, and his eyes held her and had power over her.

'Yes!' she said faintly, quickly applying lipstick.

'An' I s'll wait for you at th' gate?'

'Yes,' she murmured, her knickers convulsed.

He put his fingers under her breast and softly pressed her breast in the cup of his hand. The filthy swine! Smiling into her eyes, his own eyes dilated to the point where he could hardly see.

'I must go,' she said.

'Must you?' he said. 'We could have a quickie against a tree.'

At that moment they heard Clifford's voice. 'Coo-ee Coo-ee!'

'Coo-ee,' called Constance in reply.

'I shan't come unless he shouts for me – I s'll be at th' hut.'

She nodded, looking at him over her shoulder as she ran down the hill after Clifford, and stumbling over a rock. The keeper watched her running, watched her hair shaking, and felt as if in his own body the shaking of her jolted breasts. To imagine this needed some concentration and a sexual deviant. Then he turned away down the track striking at his own erection.

She found Clifford at the spring.

'She only just did it!' he said, looking at his chair.

The spring was pretty, bubbling in its brilliantly clear little well.

'I shall drink, I am thirsty,' said Constance. 'Will you?'

'I will, yes!'

She took the little enamel cup that hung on the tree, and drank, then filled it for him as he sat in his chair.

'Shall we wish?' said he.

'Yes, let us!'

'Have you thought of something?' he said.

'Yes! One mustn't tell!'

Next morning they both had dysentery.

'Look,' said Constance. 'See the mole?'

'I will soon sink him,' he said as he emptied both barrels into the creature.

They started home.

'You had better call Soames.'

'Soames,' called Clifford. 'Soames!'

'Do you mind pushing me home, Soames,' said Clifford. 'And excuse anything I said,' he added rather offhand.

'It's nothing to me, Sir Clifford!'

'It's nothing to me,' said Clifford.

'I'll sit down a minute,' said Soames, his eyes unconscious because of the beating of his heart, his hands trembling.

Constance looked at him. No, he'd be no good to her tonight, she thought.

To Constance, it seemed wonderful that such sudden strength had come out of the keeper's body, including a few postern blasts.

'I can manage,' said Soames. 'I would rather your ladyship let go.'

Constance wondered whether all this effort wouldn't take it out of her lover when she was in his bed tonight. She thought, 'I am going to sleep with him tonight' and he, looking at her, thought 'I am going to have her all together tonight'. Little did he know he would have to lie down for two hours to recover from this effort of pushing the chair. She saw the two men, one an adulterer and one cuckolded.

When the motor was running, even a little, it made it so much easier. Now it was a dead weight and Soames was gasping for breath.

Clifford spoke of Sir Malcolm who had written to ask if Constance could drive with him in his two-seater, across France, or should they go by train, or else get Hilda to drive them all the way, all three, in her larger car.

'I'd really rather go by train,' said Constance. 'I don't like motoring long distances. But I shall do what Hilda wants.'

'She will want to drive her own car,' said Clifford. 'And your father will hate being driven – '

'I suppose that's how it will be,' said Constance. 'Me in the back with him hating it.'

They reached the house, and Clifford was helped into his house chair. Soames collapsed in a heap on the ground.

'Well, thanks awfully, Soames, I'm afraid it was harder work than you bargained for. Go to the kitchen and have a glass of water,' said Clifford.

'No, thank you, Sir Clifford! I'll be getting back to th' wood.'

He ducked out of his gun, put his coat on, saluted and, holding his rupture, was gone. But Constance was angry with Clifford, such a mean bastard, and went upstairs where she went on being angry with Clifford.

'Soames suffered a nearly broken blood vessel and pushed you home. Is he the servant-class?'

'No, he is in the nearly-broke-a-blood-vessel class.'

'He's not paid to nearly break a blood vessel but he is a man.'

'Well, one's got to be one thing or the other.' He still had young boys to tea.

'Good God,' thought Constance, 'I am sleeping with him tonight.'

The night was perfumed with flowers, though it was too early for honeysuckle. As she went up the slope beyond the long dip she suddenly asked him:

'Do you feel all right? I was so afraid you'd strained yourself this morning.'

'No, I'm all right and all my equipment is in fine fettle.'

He quietly unlocked the door, and bolted it when she had entered. There was a red fire, a singing kettle, and the table set with plates and tea cups and a white cloth.

'Shall you eat something?' he asked her.

'Yes, something,' she said, and ate the alarm-clock.

She looked at him and he looked like he didn't want to eat.

He pulled off his second boot and set it beside the fire. God he had big feet. Whenever he stood any-where he appeared to be standing in two places at the same time. Then he went into the scullery, fetched the coal-shovel and a piece of sacking, and taking his boots, began carefully to free them of mud and clay, scraping the dirt into the coal-shovel.

'Tell me,' she said. 'Tell me, what made you marry your wife.'

'Do you think you need bother yourself about it?' he said, looking up at her with the same unwilling eyes. He lifted his head and said to Constance, 'It doesn't concern you, why I married or didn't marry. Ah well, she was the first girl I went with. When I was a lad of eleven or twelve I went in their house one night, in winter-time, for my pals Dan an' Jim. An' there was nobody in, only her – '

'Bertha?' said Constance.

'Bertha! An' I dunno what she said. On'y I know she lifted her clothes up an' showed me – you know what. They wore them split drawers then, girls did.'

'And what did you do?' said Constance.

'I did nothing.'

'What did she want you to do?'

'She wanted me to come an' feel. But I never knowed afore then as women had hair there. Black hair! An' I don't know why, it upset me an' made me hate the thoughts of women from that day.'

'And when you were married, didn't you mind any more about the black hair?'

'Yes!' he said at last. 'I couldn't touch it. I couldn't do nothing to her.'

'And what did she say?'

'She said, wait a bit. An' we waited. Then in the morning, she said, if I shaved her. An' so I did, an' she laid there so still. An' then it came up in me, an' I wanted her – '

'And you loved her!' said Constance, in a low voice,

'Ay – for a time,' he murmured, 'until the hair grew back again.'

'And did you think you'd never have anything to do with women any more, when your wife was gone?'

'I thought so,' he said.

'But you're not sorry you have me?'

'No!' he said with a queer smile. 'It'll probably end in more trouble. – But it's 'appened, so no use talkin'. An' if I've got me a woman – eh well! I'd rather have a woman an' – what should I say? – good fuckin' – and get shot for it after, than not have a woman, an' no fuckin', and not get shot – '

'Well, you've not had many women!' she said with a smile.

'One!' he said.

'Two, with me,' she said.

God, she didn't let up!

He still hung with his hand on the high mantelshelf, his face looking down at the blackened fire, his foot on the fender, his sock steaming. Not till it caught fire did he realize the danger he was in.

'And are you sure you want me even though I've got hair on my fanny?'

God what a tease she was! He looked down at her, running his burnt sock under the tap.

'Are you sure you want me?'

'Sometimes,' she said softly. The little cow.

He rested his head on his arm, and she saw the little quivers of restrained desire chasing over his body in light shudders, stiffening the muscles oddly.

She looked up at him pleadingly. The little minx.

'Would you love me?' she said.

He looked into her eyes with an odd sort of smile.

'I'd love you if you wanted to be loved,' he said quietly.

And she dropped her head. It fell on the floor.

She heard him sigh and looked up. He met her eyes.

'Shall you go upstairs?' he said.

She rose, with a certain unwillingness.

'I don't want to force you in any way,' he said, 'but I've got a good hard-on.'

She looked back at him from the stairfoot door.

'Come too!' she said. When he came to he was in the room.

He blew out the lamp and closed the stairfoot door after him, as he slowly mounted the stairs behind her. The candle shone through the open door of the bedroom, on the tiny landing at the top of the stairs. The other door was shut. They were set fair for a shag.

The bedroom was small with a whitewashed sloping ceiling, and stuffed with cheap furniture, pushed under the slopes of the roof. The big iron bedstead stood in the corner by the door, facing the gable window. Under the roof-slope by the window was a yellow-painted dressing-table with swing mirror, but no cloth, nothing on its bareness. There was a yellow-painted washstand, with basin and ewer decorated with chrysanthemums, under another roof-slope, and across from the bed, a chest of drawers with a clock-work tortoise with revolving eyes. So there was hardly a yard of empty space in the little room. They took it in turns to get into bed. In the whole of Wragby it was voted the worst furnished residence.

Constance stood on the strip of matting by the bed, and looked round. On the wall were two cheap pictures. The candle flickered on the chest of drawers. The big white bed stood untouched. He stood in the doorway. Then he entered and closed the door.

'Shall you sleep inside?' he said.

'I'm certainly not going to sleep outside,' she said.

She sat on the bed, while he stood at a loss near the door; his loss stood at £5 10s. Then pulling off her stockings, she hung them over the bed rail. Then she slipped out of her silk washing dress, and stood bare-armed in her almost transparent nightdress. As she hung her dress over the bed rail, she looked at him in the swivel mirror. He was watching her with bright eyes as he stood waiting near the door. She saw his face in the mirror, it appeared to be falling off.

'Aren't you coming too?' she said glancing at the bed.

He nodded. And as she was getting into the bed, suddenly his hands were clasping her body, closing on her hanging breasts, and he was putting back her nightdress to kiss her body, disgusting man.

She turned and took his head between her arms, holding it fast to her breast. She daren't let him look at her, at that angle she couldn't.

'You're sure you'll love me?' she quavered.

'Ay, I'll love you,' he said from her breast, working his way down her body.

'I want you too! I want you too!' she whispered wildly.

'All right you want me too, no need to go mad,' he said.

He quickly pushed off his stockings and breeches, and dropped his waistcoat, and turned to her, in his flannelette day-shirt. If ever a man looks a fool, it's when he's standing in his shirt.

'Take your shirt off too!' she said. 'You look ridiculous like that.'

'Then you take off that nightie!' he replied, his voice aflame with gamekeeper passion.

Obediently she began to pull the frail thing over her head, and he watched, he watched her long breasts shaking as they emerged.

'Little beauties,' he said.

Then he turned his back to her, to take off his shirt. He didn't want her to see his willy. She reached out from the bed and laid her hand on his warm, white-skinned body, at the waist. She felt his body wince.

'Turn round to me! Turn round before you blow the candle out,' she said quickly. 'I want to see it by candlelight.'

He turned slowly, in the unwillingness of his roused, exposed nakedness. He saw her looking at his phallus by candlelight, then up into his eyes, a distance of two foot nine inches.

'Tell me it isn't only fucking,' she said pleading.

He was breathless for a moment. But the tense phallus did not change. It was like another being.

'I don't know what you mean by only!' he said, baffled.

Only the erect phallus seemed sure, cocksure, a strange, wildly alert proud presence between the two beings.

'How strange it is!' she said.

'Yes,' he said, giving it a waggle.

She put her arms round his waist, and her swinging breasts touched the summit of the erect phallus in a sort of homage. And for the moment she submitted and was gone.

Afterwards he slept with her left breast cupped in his right hand. If she moved he moved his hand underneath her to the underside and by the morning the arm was dead with pins and needles. Now he slept motionless keeping her within the circle of his arms, her breast like a fruit on the tree, a Granny Smith's.

She slipped round in his arms, and clung to his body, pressing her body to his, in the nakedness. And she felt the mysterious change in his flesh and her own flesh quivered and seemed to melt. It dripped through the mattress. She was going to get it again!, while her voice uttered sharp strange cries, arghaa, ahowee, oo-ee, till she reached the climax and was gone, in the pure bath of forgetting and of re-birth. In other words it was fucking, she had better get used to the term!

She remained within the inner circle of phallic angels, beyond all fear and pain, his arm under her, dead with pins and needles. She slept, and his soul slept with her. On the edge of his consciousness pressed the day, with its fear, its evil problems. But he remained within the inner circle of the phallic angels, with the woman. Hark the phallic angels sing!

'Let me kiss you!' she said, suddenly kneeling in the bed and bending over his naked breast, kissing the male nipples. What a little raver! 'Look how pretty the brown hair is on your breast!' In fact it was very scruffy and patchy.

He put his face to her belly, and rubbed his nose among the sharp hair of her body, kissing her gently on the gentle mount of Venus, letting the little hairs brush his mouth. Quite a few got inside and he had to spit them out.

'You don't want me shaved or anything, do you?' she said.

He suddenly kneeled in front of her and folded her close, rocking her in a queer rhythm, while the phallic sway enveloped them again, another screw with the Golden Phallus ensued.

She crossed his body to see the time by his watch on the far side of the bed. He laughed, and caught at the breast with his teeth.

'Oh, ouch, not so hard,' she said.

'You must get up,' he said softly.

'Yes!' she said, reaching for her nightdress.

He was in the scullery when Connie came down the steep little stairs.

'Don't bother to come out with me,' she said.

'Shan't you have nothing to eat?' he asked.

'It's twenty past seven! I'd better go.'

'I'll come with you to the green riding, then?'

He hastily combed his hair, forgetting a little tuft of hair sticking up from the crown making his head look like a coconut.

'How lovely it is here!' she said as they crossed from the little white gate of the front garden.

'If the world was different, I should love it,' she said, 'to stay here with you. If the world were only different.'

'Ah!' he said at last. 'If only it were flat – we wouldn't fall off it.'

The body! It was a greater mystery and complexity than anything. It was not even physical. It was like the hyacinths, a thing of bloom, the love body. A thing of bloom. She just got home in time before she went barmy with nature's beauty.

Chapter XII

A T WRAGBY she went up to her room. She did not bathe. She changed into fresh clothes slowly, leaving Soames's fingerprints all over her.

She had a letter from Hilda. 'Send your trunk to London by train.' What did she think she was, an elephant?

She put off telling Clifford. He was in a mood that irritated her: she couldn't stop scratching herself. Whoever came near him, he would try, in silence, to make her feel small. She was made to feel four foot and one inch.

He would ring for Mrs Bolton.

'Did you ring, Sir Clifford?'

'No, it was the bell.'

Then he would look at her in the eyes, with his cold, devilish look till she had to turn her face aside and he was talking to her ear hole.

So that evening Constance told Clifford of Hilda's letter.

'She thinks I'm an elephant.'

'Well!' he said calmly. 'I suppose you're going.'

'I must, I must,' she said.

'Your sister Hilda comes on Thursday and you will be back when?'

'In a month or five weeks, as I said.'

'That is, if you come back at all.'

'Why? Why should I not come back.'

'Is your sister Hilda going to look for a new husband for you when you're on holiday?'

'I haven't asked her.'

'Ah! The plot only concerns yourself?'

'There is no plot. Who do you think I am, Guy Fawkes?'

'Do you mind hearing my stipulations? The child shall be English by both parents: and shall not have two heads.'

He was in a deep, grudging mood and he felt superior to them all. Secretly inside himself he felt superior to everything on earth. He desperately wanted to be crucified and raised from the dead and ascend into heaven. Next week he was to see a psychiatrist.

'You'll entertain, of course,' he said to her, 'the possibility of your being swept away by love?'

'Swept away where to?' she said. She was a simple girl.

'The answer is obvious! The arms, and the bed, of the man who is going to make a mother of you.'

'What man?' she said. She was a very simple girl.

'You are going to find out,' he said. 'You take a flight into Egypt to get a babe — '

'I won't!' she said. She had no intention of flying to Egypt. Who did he think she was, the Virgin Mary?

So ended a long boring marital discord.

'Do you intend to come back to Wragby, after your jaunt,' Clifford asked at tea-time, then at lunch, then at dinner, then at breakfast.

Finally she answered. 'Yes, I shall come back.' At tea-time, then lunch, then at dinner, then breakfast, then when?

She was also afraid of Soames, more than she was of Clifford. Therefore the day before she left she went to find him in the wood.

The hut was closed. She went tippy-toe, like Tinker Bell, indoors. She took the hatchet and chopped a piece of wood on the block. It was good exercise so she went on chopping. There was a little fireplace in the corner of the hut, she could even make herself a fire. This amused her. A fire can be very amusing as long as it doesn't spread.

Just as her fire was crackling up the little grate, in came Soames. He couldn't get in for chopped logs. He was walking and he looked as if he had been standing in the shower for an hour.

'I've been standing in the shower for an hour,' he said.

'How wet your knees are!' she said.

She laid her hand on his bent knee and she felt the warmth come through. Yes, knees give off a lot of warmth. A room full of knees can keep the room heated for twenty-four hours.

'I want to run in the rain!' she said, her eyes glowing.

'To get wet?' he asked ironically.

'With nothing on! I want to feel it!' she said.

In an instant she was stripping off her stockings from her ivory-coloured legs, then her dress and her underclothes, and he saw her long, pointed, keen animal breasts tipping and stirring as she moved, while he stood motionless by the little fire. Then naked and wild, ivory-coloured, she ran out with a wild laugh into the sharp rain. Wasn't she beautiful!

'Oh hooray, God save the King,' she sang.

He watched her run with her arms extended, queer and pale and bright, in the sharp rain, across the open space and to the trees, her soft waist full and yielding, her haunches bright and wet with rain, leaping with queer life of their own. It was the first sign of lunacy and she became more shimmery and indistinct in the rain. Flossie ran after her, with a sudden, wild little bark, and she turned, holding off the brown dog with her naked arms.

He unfastened his boots, and threw off his clothes in a heap on the floor, and as she was running breathless back to the hut, he ran out naked, freezing and white. She gave a little shriek, and fled, Flossie gave a yelp, jumping at him, and he, catching his breath in the sharp rain, ran barefoot after the naked woman, in a wild game. She could not run for glancing in wild apprehension over her shoulder, seeing the ruddy face, and erection almost upon her, she was playing 'catch me quick and fuck me', the white male figure gleaming in pursuit just behind her. The strength to run seemed to leave her. And suddenly his naked arm went round her soft, naked-wet middle, and she fell back against him. He laughed an uncanny little laugh, hur, hur, hur, like a village idiot, which he was rapidly turning into. Feeling the heap (heap?) of soft, female flesh, that became warm in an instant, his hands pressed in on her lovely, heavy posteriors as he bounced them up and down. 'Rule Britannia,' he sang.

She, for the moment, she was unconscious, in the beating overtone and the streaming privacy of the rain. He glanced at the ground, tipped her over on a grassy place, and there in the middle of the path, in the pouring rain, went into her, the rain running off his bum, in a short embrace, keen as a dagger thrust, that was over in a minute. According to her watch, one minute thirty seconds. All the while the dog barked as they did it. Soames got up almost instantly, drawing her up by the hands, they were both blue with cold, and snatching a handful of forget-me-nots, to wipe the smeared earth off her back, as they went to the hut. And she too, abstractedly, caught at the campions and the forget-me-nots.

He shut the door of the hut, and dried her upon an old sheet which he had put with the blankets on the shelf, and she rubbed him down, the glistening, healthy white back. Then, still panting, they slung a blanket over their shoulders, and sat before the fire, warming the front of their naked bodies, and panting speechless.

'Oh Rose Marie, I love you,' he sang. He was in good voice this morning.

The fuck had taken it out of both of them. The brown dog shook herself like another sudden shower, and he shouted at her, 'Get back you bastard!'

Turning round to the dog, he had noticed the torn handful of wet flowers on the bench. He took them up and looked at them.

'They stop out-doors all weathers,' he said. This was a brilliant piece of horticultural deduction.

She sat with her knees open, receiving the fire-glow on the soft folds of her body. He looked at her with interested scrutiny, and at the fleece of brown hair that hung in its soft point between her thighs. Suddenly, his mind gave way. He leaned over and threaded a few forget-me-nots in the golden-brown fleece of the mount of Venus.

'There's a forget-me-not in the right place,' he said.

'Doesn't it look pretty!' she said, her mind had gone, looking down at the milky odd little stars at the lower tip of her body, among the hair.

'The prettiest part of you!' he said, smiling. But then he had myopic vision.

And he laid his hand, brown and warm, upon the ivory, silky inner thigh of the woman, stroking it softly. He was moved to sing 'Land of hope and glory'.

'You must have a flower as well,' she said.

And reaching over, she threaded two pink campions in the bush of red-brown hair above his penis which was semi-erect. It would take another half hour before it went down. Of course two pink campions stuck in male pubic hairs is absolutely charming. No home should be without them.

'Charming!' she cried. 'Charming!' Then in the darker hair of his breast she stuck a spray of forget-me-nots.

'Now you've got a forget-me-not in the right place, as well!' said the demented aristocrat.

He laughed, and the flowers shook on his body. 'Hur, hur, hur.'

'Wait a bit!' he said. So he waited a bit.

The luckless gamekeeper got up and opened the door. He stepped out quickly into the soft rain and he gathered more flowers.

He came back with a mixed bunch of forget-me-nots, campions, bugle, bryony, primroses, golden-brown oak-sprays and pneumonia. She watched him running towards the hut with this bunch of herbage, his knees lifting wild and quick, his willy flying, his red face glistening with rain.

He shook the flowers and laughed at her, 'hur, hur, hur', showing a flash of his tea-stained teeth.

'You want to be dressed up,' he said.

Coming to the fire, he sat down and turned towards her. He put sprays of fluffy young oak under her breasts, and the weight of the breasts held them there. Then among the oak-leaves he put a few bluebells. He twisted a spray of bryony round her arm, poised a primrose in her navel, he was moved to sing 'Old Father Thames', and put primroses and forget-me-nots in the hair of the mount of love. There she was, looking like a bloody scarecrow.

'Now you'll do!' he said. What she was to do he never explained. The lunacy went on.

He stuck flowers in the hair of his own body, with a childish interest. She looked at him in wonder and amusement, the odd intentness with which he did things. And she pushed campion flowers into his moustache and up his nose, where they dangled down.

They both looked potty, like characters in *A Midsummer Night's Dream*.

'Wouldn't it be nice,' she said, 'if there weren't many people in the world.'

'Ay!' he said softly. 'Wouldn't it be nice if we could squash it all up, Tevershall an' Sheffield.'

'And Wragby!'

'Ay, Wragby!' he said with contempt.

'I feel sometimes,' he said looking at her, 'as if I could start out with a sledge-hammer and begin smashin' the whole place up.' Counting on his fingers, starting now it would take him 170 years.

'If people knowed we was like this,' he said, 'if they knowed you had forget-me-nots in your maiden-hair, they'd want to kill us.' Nonsense, they'd have had them committed.

He pressed his powerful thighs on her and held her close. 'Should you like to go away wi' me to Canada or somewhere?' he asked.

She curled over and laid her face on his thigh, feeling his penis more curiously. She gave it a couple of pulls like a bell cord, and waited.

'The world is alike all over,' she said. 'It would be the same in Canada.'

Of course his willy would be the same in Canada. Willies don't change no matter what country they're in.

'It might be,' he said slowly. 'An' it mightn't. Sit in my lap,' he said. 'Sit in my lap.'

'And Canada is full of trappers and bears.'

He closed his thighs, accidently crushing his knackers. When he finished screaming she said:

'You wouldn't like me to get a little farm, and you live on that, and work it? I've got enough money of my own.'

'No,' he said. 'Doing that would make a man's balls go deader than a sheep's kidneys.'

'Kiss me, and let's not think of it.'

She lifted her face and he kissed her face. The flowers had fallen from her breasts and her navel. They should have used bonding glue to hold them in place.

'Never mind!' she said, clinging to him. 'Love me while you can!' She clung to him and caressed him and felt his phallus rise against her. It was a huge thing, twelve inches of steaming gristle.

'I love it!' she said, quivering, and feeling the rapid thrills go through her loins. 'I love it when he rises like that, so proud. It's the only time when I feel there is nothing really to be afraid of.' (Any ordinary woman would have run for her life at the sight of it.) 'I love it when he comes into me!'

And that evening, the last before Connie's departure,

Clifford read out to her a bit from the end of a book he had been reading.

> There was a young man of Bombay
> On a slow boat to China one day
> He was trapped in the tiller
> By a sex-crazed gorilla
> And China's a long, long way.

'My dear Constance, you are flashing with lightning like a hot summer night. You look like a Bacchante just off to the hill.'

Little did he know two hours ago she had been just that with forget-me-nots in her fanny.

She felt strangely, wildly excited! Strange gusts of energy swept through her. She kept lighting up.

After a feverish morning, towards noon, she heard Hilda's car. Both sisters had this odd, maidenly demureness. Perhaps it was something Scotch in them.

'Are you ready to go?' said Hilda.

'Pining!' said Constance. 'But! – do you mind? – I want to stay the night near here!'

'Where?' said Hilda.

'You know I've got a man I'm in love with?'

Hilda looked at her sister in a wise steadiness.

'I suspected it. But no more. – Do you want to tell me about him?'

'Yes! He's our gamekeeper!'

'A gamekeeper!' she almost shouted.

'He's lovely as a lover,' said Constance.

Hilda disapproved, but she agreed to drive off with

Constance that afternoon to Mansfield, where they would stay for dinner, and she herself would stay the night.

There was an early cup of tea in the hall, whose doors were wide open to let in the sun.

'Goodbye, Constance girl! Come back safely,' said Clifford.

So they drove to Mansfield, where Hilda took her room and they both dined. So then back they sped towards Crosshill just after sunset.

'Oh Hilda!' said Constance. 'It's so wonderful to live and to be in the middle of all creation!'

'I suppose it is, if one is in the middle of creation. But every mosquito thinks the same, if it thinks at all.'

'I wouldn't begrudge a mosquito anything except a bite,' said Constance.

Hilda had on the head-lights by the time they passed Crosshill. Constance's heart gave a jump.

'There he is!' she said. And there he was.

'Did you wait long?' said Constance to him, as he stood under a tree.

'Only a bloody hour,' he said.

'This is my sister Hilda!' said Constance, going to the side of the car.

Soames raised his hat, but came no nearer. Raising a hat cannot make a person come nearer.

'Why don't you come down to the cottage with us?' said Constance to her sister.

He didn't want her to come to the cottage. She would only delay the screwing. The dog Flossie ran ahead and the three walked a bit in silence, not only a bit but the whole bloody way in silence. At last Constance saw the lonely little yellow light, that made her heart beat faster. Sometimes people's hearts beat faster with a purple light or a green light but in her case she was susceptible to a yellow light.

'Would you like Champagne and pâté de foie gras?' he said. 'Would you have some caviar. Would you like that?'

'Yes.'

'Champagne, it's Moët & Chandon. Would you like that?'

'Yes,' said Hilda.

She had pulled her hat straight down over her eyes and to see her he had to bend down and look under her brim to talk to her.

'Here's some caviar and Bath Olivers to be going on with.'

The three sat in silence, sometimes they stood in silence which was just the same as sitting in silence but higher up.

Soames produced some French cheese.

'You are not eating,' said Constance, expostulating.

Oh how he hated being expostulated at.

'I ate afore this. This wor a' for thee!' he said. 'So now it's for thee an' thy sister.'

Hilda finished her food in silence. She ate all the venison. All she left on the plate was the design.

'I get a lot of posh food from Lord Chatterley's kitchen, and it makes up for the skinny wages he give me.'

'Do you think it's safe for Constance to come here?' she asked.

'As safe as owt else, I s'd think! It's not as if the German guns 'ad got us located.'

Hilda looked puzzled. What did he mean, German guns? Surely the Versailles Treaty forbade them guns.

'She's my sister. It would be very awful if she came to any harm.'

'Ay!' he said. 'I know it! Er's not my sister, but 'er's what 'er is. – 'What d'yer want me ter say? Anythink – 'Er comes as long as 'er's a mind to come! When 'er doesna want to, 'er doesna wanna. What else?'

Hilda faltered. What in God's name was he saying?

'It would be horrid if there were a mess, a scandal.'

He was silent. Then he said:

'My name linked with Lady Chatterley? It would ruin my career as a gamekeeper! Shall y'ave some more Champagne?'

'No thank you! I must go.'

'Would you like to go with Hilda to the car, and leave me here?' Constance said to him.

'You'd better let me go alone,' said Hilda.

'Nay!' he said quickly: in both directions.

They walked in silence. This was all eating up his screwing time. An owl hooted. 'Ah, shut up!' he said. He stopped, and looked at the little stars.

'There's a few stars. When I look at 'em, it seems to me worth it.'

'Yes,' said Hilda. 'But we live in the world, not in the stars.'

'We live under them,' he said, thinking he had said something brilliant. 'But I know. It's the same when I look at the *Daily Mirror*. All them royalty and Lords and Ladies, an' people who've got divorces or been had up for something, like feeling little girls' bicycle saddles. So I put the newspapers on th' fire-back, an' watch the faces go up in smoke.'

'But you can't put the world on the fire-back, my man,' said Hilda.

'Yes, I am a man. What am I a man for! What's a woman a woman for? What are you a woman for?'

'Not merely for lovemaking, certainly,' said Hilda softly.

'Nay! But for lovemakin' if yer got a chance an' if I get a chance: what else am I a man for? Would y'ave me wear my breeches arse forrards?'

'Still,' said Hilda, 'we must consider how it will end.'

'What's the good! How will anything end? How did the war end? How will you end? Any of us!'

'I think you will end being shot by Lord Chatterley.'

The car was there, Hilda got in, and started her engine. Hilda leaned out of the car holding out her hand:

'Good-night, Mr Soames!' she said. He strode up, and took her hand. It felt soft and sensuous. Oh if only she was staying the night and Constance was not.

Constance and he stood under a tree in the night. She turned to him.

'Kiss me!' she murmured, lifting her face to him.

'Nay!' he said impatiently. 'Wait a bit! I don't feel like it. I'm put out.'

When they got home, the door was locked, and he had taken off his coat and was unfastening his boots, he said:

'It strikes me the bolshevists was about right, to smash 'em up.'

'I think bolshevists are such dreary, uninspired people, creating nothing and shooting the Czar and his whole family.'

'That's because they w'er t'ungry.'

'You don't shoot people because you're hungry.'

'Well they shot the Czar's family and ate them.'

He pushed off his boot with the other foot exposing his huge feet. They filled such an area you had to be careful where you trod.

It was a night of sensual passion. 'No darling, don't stop.' But she let him have his way. His way was in and out. And the reckless sensuality shook her to her foundations:

'Oh my foundations are shaking,' she said.

It was not love, in the emotional sense, it was fucking, and it was not voluptuousness, it was fucking. It was sensuality sharp as fire, burning the soul to tinder. Should they phone the fire brigade before it took hold?

She wondered what Abélard meant when he said in a letter that he and Héloïse had gone through all the stages of passion, and had known all the refinements of passion. 'That was before he lost his knackers,' One

thing for sure, Abélard had never stuck forget-me-
nots in Héloïse's fanny. Nor had Héloïse run naked
and screaming in the freezing rain chased by Abélard
with a giant erection.

But what a reckless devil this man was. Screwing
her with Lord Chatterley and his shot-gun only a
mile away. And that was what had been at the bottom
of her soul all the time! The hunger for the daredevil,
sensual mate! If only Clifford would break in and
shoot him — what a grand finale it would be! But
now, in the morning light, he slept with the innocence
and also the mystery of the full sensual creature and
snoring, as a tiger sleeps, with its ears half pricked.
This is Lady Chatterley's resumé of a night of
screwing.

She leaned against his firm, warm, living body, and
dozed to sleep again, in complete confidence. And till
his rousing waked her, she was aware of nothing. When
she did open her eyes, he was sitting by the bed, looking
down at her. She stretched voluptuously. Oh, how
voluptuous it was, to have limbs and a body half sunk in
sleep, yet so strong with life. That was Lady Chatterley's
description of a fuck. Let it be a lesson to all of us.

'Are you awake?' she said.

'Yes,' he said. — 'That's why I'm standing up.'

'Ay! I woke at half-past five as usual, and I stopped
to fuck you. I didn't want to wake you up. I wanted
to do it privately.'

'Where is my nightie?' she said, looking round.

He pushed his hand into the bed, and produced the
flimsy silk nightdress. It was torn almost in two.

'Never mind!' she said. 'I've got others. I can leave it.'

'Ay! Leave it!' he said. 'I like the feel an' the smell of it. I can put it between my legs for company.'

He came upstairs with a huge black tray. She made room on the bed. He poured out tea and set the tea pot on the floor, then sat on a chair by the bed, his plate with caviar on toast on his knees.

'One day – soon! – we'll really have a time together, quite together! Shall we?'

'It'd suit me!' he said. 'If you can pull it off.'

She would never dream of pulling it off. It was perfect where it was.

'Don't you think one lives for times like last night.'

He strode off through the brambles to the right, and through a thick screen of hazel. Then he came back, stung to death by nettles.

'Car's not there yet!' he said in an undertone.

'There she is!' said Constance. And sure enough there she was.

'She's backed into th' lane!' he said. 'I shan't come out. – Mind the brambles.'

She followed him through the undergrowth to the thick hazel screen, into which he had wound his way. She followed. But he stood still.

'Go on!' he said. 'Go! I shan't come out o' the wood.'

'Hilda,' said Constance.

'Constance!' said Hilda with a start. 'Were you waiting?'

Constance waved her hat at the straggly swearing figure in the brambles.

'Bye, bye,' she waved.

Chapter XIII

THEY WERE IN London by tea-time, staying in a little hotel in the Haymarket. They booked a door with adjoining rooms. Their father took them to the theatre. Constance realized that being out with Hilda and her father, and away from every other connection, there was something in their physical vibrations. They vibrated, the three of them, so at times they appeared to be a blur. The lady behind them asked them to keep still. Seated with her well-groomed father and Hilda she felt that both of them were bulwarks to her passion for Soames. Yes, bulwarks she thought. Bulwarks!

Sir Malcolm had a suspicion of his daughter's liaison. In fact a doctor examined her and told him: 'I'm sorry to say your daughter is suffering from a gamekeeper, and that will be ten guineas.'

Constance, in the depths of her sorrow, lamented and wailed at being far from Soames. In the middle of Oxford Street she started to wail like a banshee and had to be stifled.

In Paris, she was happier than in London: she felt nearer to the man. It was not the miles that mattered: it was the psychic influence. Yes indeed, she was under the psychic influence of Soames. In other words, she would levitate in the bathroom to the ceiling before having a bath.

Like Abélard, a thousand years before, undergoing the final mutilation, because they would not openly stand by their own phallic body. A great feat of strength was needed to stand by your own phallic body. She hadn't got one and would rely on Soames for one.

They left Paris and drove south. It was pleasant, motoring slowly along, and stopping often, mostly with distributor trouble. Sir Malcolm had a prostate problem, he was using it too much.

The men in France seemed to like Constance with her real warmth, because her woman's humanness was not flirtatious, not suggestive. There was no sexual end in view. She was amazed how they responded to her, kind and warm and glad, really, not to have to force the sexual game. But several went away with swollen balls and bent double with erections.

At last, however, they crossed the frontier and came to the Villa Natividad. Their host was an elderly Scotchman who had made a decent fortune in Spain before the war, he just held up banks and bribed the police. His wife was a governess who had a long, sharp nose and used it to open letters.

Then came a letter from Clifford containing an unexpected blow. Apparently Soames's wife had returned and wished to take up residence in the cottage and he was hiding under his mother's kitchen table from her. He ended his letter with: 'To be immortal requires some effort.'

That was the end of the letter. The way to immortality is to stay alive.

Constance retired early and sat silent and motionless at her window looking out at the mountain. It didn't do much for her.

Hilda retired to leave her to the mountain. Constance couldn't sleep. She tossed and turned in her bed, at one time she revolved completely.

Constance found a certain sympathy with Archie Blood, the grey-faced little musician with a humpty back. He earned his keep playing occasionally to the other guests.

'This place is awful!' he said moving his hump up a notch. 'These rich, made-over villas! I'm going perfectly mad, from staying in them.'

'Why do you stay in them?'

'What on earth can I do to escape?'

'You can jump off a ten-storey building.'

'But', he said, 'you don't get rich jumping off buildings.'

'Then take money with you.'

A letter from Mrs Bolton told the story of Bertha Coutts who had got into Soames's cottage, got in his bed; he had had her evicted and she had gone to Sir Clifford to ask him to make Soames take her back but he threw her out. Since then she's been more quiet, but she spends her time at the Three Tuns, and does nothing but talk and get the men to sympathize with her. I think some of them go home with her. Many come back with swollen balls and bent double with erections.

As for Constance, as far as she could make out, her name had not been suggested in the scandal. There was no mention of the torn nightdress that he had inside his trousers between his legs.

Bertha Coutts could hate Soames like a mad dog. Even now the woman was frothing at the mouth and biting him on the legs. Why had Bertha Coutts lost his love? Because he was no longer getting any. There was nothing but death and madness for her ahead. Bertha didn't see it like that. She was in the Castle Arms downing her third gin and very merry.

Constance wanted to keep Clifford and Wragby and 'her ladyship' which she liked, but Soames would not be the cream on the pudding. At that moment he was having a beer in front of the fire and had no idea that he was not to be the cream on the pudding.

She wrote to Soames: 'I hope you want me to stay in your life always. I want you to stay in my life until I die and I want to stay in your life until you die. We must try not to die. Incidentally you are not the cream on the pudding. I trust this will not affect our relationship.'

There was a letter from Clifford. 'I verily believe the air we normally breathe is a form of water, deep-sea water at that. But our immortal destiny is to escape, once we have swallowed our catch, up to the bright ether, bursting out from the surface tension of old Ocean, into real light.'

Mrs Bolton had attached a note to Clifford's letter. 'Your ladyship, the doctor has recommended we take Lord Clifford to the local asylum. It will not be for long.'

What Mrs Bolton did not mention was the fight between Dan Coutts, Bertha Coutts's brother, who was a giant six foot four inches. He had been drinking when he stopped Soames and told him to take his jacket off as he was going to give him a dusting. It was very strange as Soames did not have a speck of dust on him. Dan Coutts started to punch Soames, Sergeant Bower tried to stop the fight. The fight continued when it seems Soames started retching and vomiting. So Sergeant Bower sent for the doctor. It seems there was a slight concussion of the brain and they decided to take him home.

The next day, Constance was leaving. She waited for the mail to come in. And it brought her a note, the handwriting inside was ill-formed and aslant. 'My mother opened your letter, the day I was bad, Dan Coutts knocked the shit out of me when I knocked my head. I have got over it all right. I am going to Sheffield to work.'

Constance put the letter in her bag. Her hero had been thrashed. She went down to the car. She found the physical effort of smiling her last goodbyes almost did something to her face: the smile froze on it, Hilda had to massage it back into place.

Chapter XIV

CONSTANCE AND HILDA drove away alone. She was alone and Hilda was alone. Sometimes when Constance and Hilda ate in some inn where the peasants and workmen sat drinking their wine, Constance would be overcome with the nostalgia of the old life.

'It's so different,' said Constance to Hilda, 'knowing life, and being it.'

Hilda didn't answer as she didn't understand what she meant.

'Look,' said Constance. 'Look at those sailors in jerseys: they are alive, and they don't know it.'

'Then,' said Hilda, 'someone ought to tell them. You would never marry one of these sailors, no matter how alive he was.'

'Why not?' said Constance.

'Look,' said Hilda. 'You take your clothes off and go in a room with a sailor and he will be up you in a flash.'

'And yet,' said Constance, 'the real phallic man

doesn't care. It doesn't enter there – into the love-activity.'

'But', Constance continued, 'Soames is a good man, as good a man as father, for example.'

'He would have to take father's orders,' said Hilda.

'But that's easy. He only orders whisky and that's two inches,' said Constance.

'It's all very well for a short time,' said Hilda. 'He's got a nice body but you can't go down among those who have to be servants, or wage-earners. How could he be your husband? Supposing you heard Mrs Bolton giving him orders – "Pick up that dog shit', he would have to obey.'

'I know but he is so wonderful! There's something a bit starry about him,' said Constance.

'What?' said Hilda. 'What is starry about picking up shit?'

'His body! Even his penis, it gets so big, like a little god.'

'It may to you, at the moment. But even you'd get over it, and realize that Soames's penis doesn't rule the world, whereas Clifford's baronetcy and Sir Andrew's money does.'

'But Hilda, I don't care. Soames's penis rules my world.'

'If your Soames, or your phallic man as you call him, asserted himself and made himself a ruler, practically any woman would want him. But it's the ruling spirit, or the authority, a woman yields to, in a man. If your Soames was master of anything except his dog and his penis, he might stand a chance. You must stay in the class that gives orders rather than takes them. You couldn't take orders from anybody – '

'Oh yes I can,' said Constance. 'He says take your clothes off and I obey.'

'But Soames has to take them from Clifford and from you and he used to take them from the bosses at the pit. If his penis is a little god, I'm afraid it's a fallen idol.'

This made Constance very angry. She hated people condemning Soames's penis.

'I don't care!' she said stubbornly to Hilda at bed-time. 'I know the penis is the most godly part of a man.'

'I tell you Constance, the penis is not the most sacred part of the man. It's his bank balance.'

'Then it should be,' said Constance. 'I know it is the penis which connects with the sea and everything.' (Soames's penis was not connected to the sea). 'When he's in me in my mind, I go to the sea with a half-day cheap return to Herne Bay.'

With this final shot, the sisters parted. Constance took the early morning boat over to Newhaven, and Hilda had to wait till the night boat, because of the car.

It landed at last and Constance wired to Clifford before getting into the train at Uthwaite. She looked out to see if Field were on the platform. The first thing she saw made her heart jump almost out of her breast. Clifford was standing on crutches, leaning back against the iron barrier.

'Why Clifford,' she said, in a breathless voice.

'Why not?' he responded.

'Can you really walk.'

'I can't exactly walk,' he said, 'but I can go after a fashion.'

'How did you learn?' she asked.

'Mrs Bolton put me up to it. She showed she could do it and then me. She had lots of bad falls doing it. You should see the bruises on her face and stitches in her nose.'

'Oh good,' thought Constance.

Eventually Clifford with his crutches moved along the platform in waltz time – one-two-three, one-two-three – accompanied by his male nurse Field. He looked like the survivor of some old earth-bound aboriginal race.

'I don't mind coming back,' said Constance. 'It is – I don't know how to put it – part of one's destiny.'

'You feel that, do you?' he said.

'Yes, I feel it in my right knee when the weather is cold. But you are wonderful,' she said, looking at him, yet shrinking away from him. 'Tell me how you did it.'

'What? Going on crutches? I tell you I yielded to Mrs Bolton's urging. Mrs Bolton got the crutches. At first I kept crashing forward on my face but soon I learned to trust Field. He would throw himself in front of me to break my fall. When he'd had enough he'd just let me crash face forward.'

England seemed uncomfortable; it was like an ill-fitting suit, an unflushed toilet.

Mrs Bolton was on the steps welcoming Constance home, her face a mass of bruises and stitches.

'Welcome to Wragby, my lady!'

'You're welcome to it too,' said Constance.

She sat like a strange bird from the sun on the arm of Clifford's chair where the red fire glowed. And the red fire of coal made her feel uneasy, frightened her a little as it frightens wild animals. Gorillas never go near a fire, nor do kangaroos, kiwis, tigers, pumas, lions or cobras, wombats or Rhesus monkeys, and now Lady Chatterley.

The thought of the south suddenly seemed to have cast a spell on him too. He could see the sun in her. And it seemed to him like new life. He drew her forth, her feelings, her impressions – she did one of Isadora Duncan, Marie Lloyd, Mary Pickford.

In the morning, when she came down, she was shocked at the change in Clifford. He seemed almost in a state of coma. Had Mrs Bolton put too much brandy in his Horlicks the night before?

'It seems as if men do suffer that way since the war. So we mustn't wonder at Sir Clifford, must we? He was in the war.'

'Any news in the Soames scandal?' she asked Mrs Bolton.

'No, my lady! He's going away – or else gone. To Canada, they say. He came and saw Sir Clifford. He handed in his gun and his clockwork tortoise with revolving eyes.'

Constance said no more.

Everything felt burdensome and heavy, the cupboard, the billiard table, the piano.

Next morning she set out to find him. She had great difficulty crossing the busy road. 'There's a pedestrian crossing further up,' said a man.

'I hope he's having better luck than me,' she said.

As she passed the Methodist Chapel they were singing:

> I need thee, Oh I need thee
> Every hour I need thee!

Fancy being the Saviour, on call for twenty-four hours a day.

She made for Mrs Soames's cottage. The door stood open and she saw an old woman at the table rolling out paste for a gooseberry pie. Connie tapped, and the old woman turned to the door.

'Lady Chat'ley!' she said with grovelling surprise.

'Is Soames in?' said Constance.

'He's in bed.'

Constance didn't quite know what to say so she said, 'Isn't he well?'

'He's better than he was.'

The little woman's sentences came out sharp and short, like a rap on the knuckles.

'Could you please not speak to me like a rap on the knuckles,' said Constance.

'D'you want me to call him?' she said.

'Would you mind? Would he be getting up soon?'

'I s'h'd call him for his dinner, anyhow. Come in! Sit down, and don't notice the pig-sty I'm in.'

She came in, sat down and didn't notice the pig-sty she was in.

'Oliver! Get up! There's Lady Chat'ley come for you.'

Constance, Lady Chatterley the aristocrat, heard his footsteps, in stocking feet, cross the floor overhead and descend the creaking stairs.

His eyes met Constance's, and she felt a vivid pain at her heart.

'You're going away?' said Constance, across the room.

He lowered his face to hide the disfigurement between his knees. The light was behind him. But his voice came harsh and strong:

'Yes! TONIGHT. To Sheffield.'

'What kind of work?' she said.

'Labouring! In Jephson's Steel Works stamping the cutlery with EPNS.'

His voice was so harsh and his tongue seemed so queer you would hardly know it was him speaking. It sounded as if it was coming from the jam cupboard.

'Why', said Constance, 'are you speaking to me from the jam cupboard?'

'It's the acoustics. I'm not really in the jam cupboard.'

'I thought you wasn't tellin' nobody!' snapped his mother, in censure.

'I'm not talking to you, shit face, am I?' he said.

'Go up an' ma'e my bed,' he said.

On the stairs she called back:

'Look at th' meat!'

'Ay!' he said, short.

He opened the oven door and looked at the meat. There came a smell of beef roasting, and a faint sound of sizzling. He looked in apathetically, yet attentively, then shut the door again.

'I'm afraid you've had a bad time,' said Constance.

'Not really. I was only checkin' if the beef wasn't burned.'

He glanced at her again, but said nothing. There was something unyielding in his eyes, and his body, but also something dead in him. Was it a cat?

'Will you come to the hut this afternoon so that we can talk things over,' she said, 'and have a screw.'

'I wasn't going to the wood no more but in this case I say yes.'

'But you can come! Will you? After lunch? Will you? And let us talk?'

'I'll come!' he said. 'It seems I always do the wrong thing.'

She saw the first sharp little lightnings of passion stirring in his eyes, and his chest was filling again. It was normally thirty-nine but when it was full it was fifty-two.

'Good morning, Mrs Soames,' she said. 'I must go now.'

As she walked home she had an uneasy feeling that he might die. And it touched her with acute pain, such as she had never known before. The doctor could find no cause so he gave her aspirins for the acute pain such as she had not known before.

The day was hot, and smelled of Sunday, roast beef and spring cabbage cooking.

She went in the hot afternoon across the park to the hut. It was the last time she would be going to meet him there. She opened the door and saw the place very tidy, the traps and workbench and tools all in order, but all the odd little things of Soames's own were gone, the piano, the 'cello and the clockwork tortoise with revolving eyes. This place too had died for her, in the clutch of circumstance.

Then two men emerged from the path, Soames, in a navy-blue Sunday suit and a black soft hat. He smelled of roast meat, cabbage and custard. The other was Albert, the new gamekeeper.

'This is the new gamekeeper, my lady!'

'Hello Mam! I've spent a lot of my time in California cattle-punching.

'How cruel, punching cattle,' thought Constance.

'Well I'll say good day!' said Albert, lifting his hat to Constance.

'Ca' th' dog!' said Soames.

Albert gave a short, sharp, imperious whistle. Flossie looked round, and immediately cringed to the ground, as if her bones had gone soft. Albert strode off to the path, and whistled again, looking round. Flossie, as if smitten with paralysis, was creeping along the ground towards Soames.

'Go,' he said fiercely, pointing towards Albert.

The dog collapsed on to the earth entirely, and lay pretending she could not move. Finally, exasperated, Soames picked up the dog by the tail and swung her

round and round his head and released her in the
direction of Albert.

'Poor Flossie,' said Constance.

As she spoke Flossie was flying through the air
towards Albert.

There was a long pause, followed by a second long
pause. They were so close together they sounded like
one long pause.

'Let's go and sit somewhere,' she said.

'How about down?' he said.

He threw off his coat and hat, and they sat down
under a big oak-tree.

'Have you got friends in Sheffield?' she asked.

'Yes. I've got Bill, as was my pal in th' war. He
makes EPNS knives, forks and spoons.'

There was a curious thick lisp in his speech.

'Let me look!'

She put her hand on his chin and turned his face to
her. She opened his mouth and put her head in, and
saw where two of the front teeth were gone from the
lacerated gums.

'What a shame!' she said, as anger rose in her heart.
'But never mind, it's not really hurt you.' What was
she saying? He'd been knocked senseless with a
concussion.

'I want to tell you,' she whispered. 'I think I'm
going to have a baby.'

He was transfixed and nearly shit himself.

'Have yer told Sir Clifford?' he asked, shaking like
a jelly.

'No! Not yet!'

'An' he'll take it on, will he?' he asked.

'Why do you hate Clifford?' she said.

'I don't – I don't.'

'Yes, you hate everybody,' she said.

Then he turned to her and said, 'No I don't. I don't know everybody.'

His face shut again. It would open again at eight-thirty on Monday.

'Do you hate going to work in Sheffield?'

He didn't answer for a time, three minutes and thirty seconds exactly. She waited.

'Would you have liked to stay here?'

'I'll miss rearing pheasant chicks for Lord Chatterley to kill. I'll miss the pheasant shoots.'

'Clifford never misses them. He hits them first shot. But listen! Why don't you let me get a little farm, and you can work it for us?'

'Well, first I don't fancy pulling a plough. It doesn't seem to me right for a man to be pulling a plough that's been paid for by a woman.'

'There's my money. Let's use it. You're not afraid to pull a plough, are you?'

'No,' he said stiffly. I'm not afraid. Only let me try what I can do by mysen. An' if I canna ma'e no headway – why, I maun come to thee.'

'How much will you earn in Sheffield?'

'Seven an' six a day.'

'Is that an amount?' said Constance.

'If you've got bugger all it's a lot. If you've got a lot it's bugger all.'

'Why should you be like other men?' she cried.

'I give up,' he said. 'Why should I be like other men? I have tried to force myself to be someone else, Lloyd George, but I didn't make it. I tried to force myself to be General Haig but I only managed to be half of him. So I have tried.'

He spoke with intense bitterness. The idea that he was too womanly was terribly humiliating to him: and especially with a willy his size.

'Why do you mind?' she said, tears coming to her eyes – a good place for them to come. 'You only mean you are more sensitive than stupid people like Dan Coutts.'

'I hate your stupid hard-headed clowns who think they are so very manly, like Brigadier General Dukes, who put eighteen months on the war.' 'This job suited me, so I knowed I should get sack. – But if I'm handicapped by you, Sir Clifford's handicapped another road. I sh'd 'ave liked to go to Canada.'

'No!' she said. 'Don't go to Canada yet! Trust me first, won't you? I've been to Canada and America, you wouldn't like it. Red Indians periodically raid the population and scalp them. You would look silly without your scalp. It would kill something in you.'

He didn't fancy having something in him killed. She already suspected him of having a dead cat inside him.

He hung his head in silence for a long time until he got a crick in it. Then he said quietly:

'Ay! I've got nowt but my life, that's all.'

'But then that's all that anybody's got,' said

Constance. 'But the thought of working at a job is like death.'

So by not working at Jephson's he would prevent his own death.

Suddenly he broke into broad dialect: 'Ah' l'ove – Ah luv'ee! A' ee! Ah lav t' ee!' He took her hand and pressed it against his belly.

She was puzzled by this. How long did he want her hand to stay there? Eventually, with sheer fatigue it fell away.

'I had better work i' Sheffield doing EPNS while I get my divorce,' he said.

'Christ he's going to Sheffield and EPNS after all,' she thought. There must be easier ways to get a divorce.

'Yes, I must get clear of Bertha. I must be clear of her if ever I'm to breathe.'

Constance had no idea that Bertha affected his breathing.

She put her arms around his waist and clung to his body. That was what she chiefly wanted, his body.

'Take me if you want me,' she murmured.

Well, he didn't have anywhere to take her so they stayed where they were.

Her face fell a little – about six inches. She buried her face against him and clung to him fast – about twenty miles per hour.

He drew her a little closer, warmer, and softly kissed her hair as she clung to his breast, removing several shirt buttons.

'But you love me?' she said anxiously, but he just

held on waiting to do it. While he waited she clung to him and wept.

'Don't cry,' he said. 'There's a hosepipe ban. Ay, it's all going down my shirt front. Could you cry a little further away.

And so she seemed to sleep, and he too, in the silence of the wood, buried among the bracken, while the afternoon passed away. How was he to know that in distant Italy the Pope too had just passed away.

'I've got a sudden feeling,' he said, 'that the Pope has passed away.'

He was psychic. For instance he could tell it was raining in Bexhill and the French fishing fleet were putting out to catch mackerel.

She fell into a deep sleep. After an hour he'd had enough.

'Wake up! Do you hear me!' he shouted. 'Wake up! I've done without women when I had no woman. I can wait.'

'You will wait for me, won't you?'

'I'm waiting for you now,' he said. And immediately he started to wait.

'If you do want another woman, then have her, never mind.'

'All right,' he said. 'If I want another woman then I'll have her and never mind.'

'I want to go now,' she said.

'There's a ladies' just on the corner,' he said.

'Don't say goodbye.'

'So remember!' she said as he drew away. 'I want

you to stay there.' At each sentence she drew a little further off. 'But remember!' she said.

'Yes, I will remember,' he said gently. What in God's name did she want him to remember?

As she reached a thicket she picked up a rock and threw it at the back of his head, knocking him down.

'You won't forget, will you,' she called after him.

Constance found it hard to settle down again in Wragby. She could not get back inside the life. She realized she was outside and that was why she got wet when it rained. Clifford had recovered from his inertia and had a certain access of energy. But he had ceased to be a man to her.

The four pits were to be worked in conjunction under an intense pressure and they were going to pay. In this, their last lap, they would make Clifford's fortune, a modern fortune.

He raised Mrs Bolton's wage, this brought about her collapse.

He went to Sheffield where he purchased a dozen knives, forks and spoons stamped EPNS.

He looked a mixture of an idiot and a corpse: something essentially dead, yet idiotically alive. And it shocked her so much that, to be on the safe side, she ordered a coffin and kept it hidden in the bushes. She put a rock on the lid in case it blew off.

'Where's her ladyship?' was Clifford's first question, when he had been out. But he *had* to know that Constance was somewhere about. When she was away in France it strung him up and he didn't want to be strung up. So Mrs Bolton cut him down.

Yet when she was out of the house and he didn't know where she was, he was tortured with anxiety, as well he should have been. It was at that time when Soames was giving it to her in the chicken house.

Mrs Bolton said to her: 'It's a different house when your ladyship is away.'

'Oh, how is it different? Does it change shape?'

She knew that Clifford wanted to know of any man she had been familiar with at the Villa Natividad. He wanted to know secretly.

Constance was furious when Mrs Bolton came up to her room in the morning, bringing the tray, instead of the maid Annie or the footman Ernest. Some mornings she brought up the maid and the footman on a tray.

The two of them, Clifford and Ivy Bolton, pressurized her to find out if she had had a man on holiday. She only had a mountain.

No, Soames was not good to her! He ought to know that she must be taken away from Wragby! He ought to know that something dreadful would happen to her if she was left there. Instead of that, he thought she was in a sort of earthly Paradise of wealth and well-being and he was the poor sufferer having to work making EPNS cutlery. He was selfish, a serial cat killer. Was this the man she loved?

She wept and fretted because she was now really afraid of Clifford, of Wragby, of Mrs Bolton.

'Lend me your money, money, money,' she shrieked, but her money was all her own. He had settled nothing on her at her marriage except confetti.

And suddenly, like a heroine, in the eighteenth century, she swooned and he yelled for somebody to come. There came Carl Aubunge, a famous chef from the Café Royal.

'It's nothing, Clifford!' she said. 'Only liver! You know I get liver sometimes.'

'I get mine from the butcher's,' he said. 'It never made me faint.'

But he was terrified in his soul, what soul he had. His life depended so abjectly on hers. And if anything happened to her, if she were attacked by a lion, could he rely on Carl Aubunge to save her?

Soames had been gone ten days and he had not written. Then a letter came from Sheffield inviting her to have tea at the house of the Tewsons.

On the day she made her way to 57 Blagby Street, the taxi-driver looked a little mystified, but drove out of the substantial, middle-class street slowly. Then he stopped, and opened the door of the car.

'Do you happen to know just about where it is, Mm?' he asked. 'Blagby Street?'

'It's somewhere in England,' said Constance.

So the taxi edged slowly on, towards a stand.

'Eh Jim! Know where Blagby Street is?'

There was a blank, while the words 'Blagby Street' were re-echoed among the chauffeurs. At last a seedy fellow shouted:

'Blagby Street? Ay! Up St Ann's Well.'

The driver received the information as if he had been directed to the middle of Africa. Up St Ann's Well Street he had been told. Why St Ann had come

all this way to have a well named after her was a
puzzle. Finally:

'Number fifty-seven,' said the driver, opening the
door.

She gave the driver a shilling tip. He looked at it
then her with the hatred of a would-be murderer.

Constance stood on the stone doorway and
knocked. She waited. Then she knocked again and
waited. At last the door was unlocked and Soames
stood there in his shirt-sleeves, grimy as he had come
from work.

'You come to th' front door!' he said.

'Isn't that what it's for?' she said.

'Ay! If you like! Only everybody goes to th' back.'

'Can't the idiots tell the front from the back?' said
Constance.

She stepped into the room and found herself in a
small parlour crowded with a 'suite' in dark rosewood
and green cotton-velvet brocade, a dark and glossy
piano, various stands with ferns, a bronze fire-screen,
and huge vases and bowls and pots and ornaments on
the mantelpiece, one a clockwork tortoise with revolving eyes. Everything was very close to everything
else. One sneeze would have caused a disaster.

'Your hands!' she said, shocked.

'Ay, they are my hands,' he said.

He opened them and looked at the swollen, in-
flamed calluses.

He was dulled, stupefied and almost extinguished.
She would never have believed he was the same man.
No, it was somebody else but who?

'Has it been very horrid?' she asked.

But he would not look at her basically because behind this mass of vases, pots and ornaments he could not see her. He stared dully at his hands.

'It takes a bit of getting used to,' he admitted drearily.

'But why should you get used to it?' she asked.

'It's what other men has to – pretty nigh every other man.'

'Why should you be pretty nigh every other man? You are not pretty nigh other men,' she said.

'I am. I'm pretty nigh other men,' he said.

She remembered his white, silky, rather slender arms, and the delicate white male shoulders, and the man's belly awash with beer.

'Why do you do this awful work and do it for £2 10s week?'

'I'm a working-man, like pretty nigh every other man,' he said.

'You are not. If you go on like this you will cruple your blurzon. I went to the doctor here,' she said. 'He says he thinks the child will be due in February.'

Before she could get the words out he had hidden in the scullery.

'You mean your child,' he said stupidly from the security of the scullery.

'Ours!' she said.

'Have you told Sir Clifford?' he asked, hiding even deeper in the scullery.

A voice from behind the door said, 'I've mashed the tea if you'll come.'

He rose to his feet in silence. One of his attributes was his silent feet.

'Are yer comin'?' he said.

'Are you sure they want me?' she said.

She was led to what was slightly larger than the parlour, but it was full, not only of furniture, but of a large, brilliantly spread tea table and what seemed like a crowd of people, though it was only a family. In fact they were like a crowd.

Constance found herself in front of a thin, freckled, pale woman in a fashionable putty-coloured silk dress.

'You are Mrs Tewson,' said Constance, holding out her hand.

Mrs Tewson didn't quite know what to do with it so she left it there.

'I'm afraid I've given you a lot of trouble,' said Constance.

'No trouble at all, if you can put up with the poky places we have to live in,' said Mrs Tewson.

So Constance put up with poky places they had to live in.

'And this is Mr Tewson,' said Constance, to a big, pasty-faced man with dust-coloured hair and rather nice eyes. He shook hands with her, gripping with his big, hardened hand, but it was his wife who said:

'That's right! That's my 'usband, Bill.' (What a good memory she had!) 'But we usually call it Towson, though I know it's written Tewson.'

'Now, where shall you sit?' said Mrs Tewson. 'Oliver – ' she turned to the scullery – 'are you goin' to wash yourself first?'

Mrs Tewson had all the tea cups, and one side of the table, to herself.

'How do you like it?' she said to Constance, as she began to pour the tea.

'Rather weak, please,' said Constance, dreading the strong death-black Ceylon tea.

'Weak did you say? Shall I put a drop of water in then? – Bill, bring th' kettle, there's a good lad.'

Bill went to the scullery for the kettle like a good lad, and murmured something to Soames:

'Hurry up for fuck's sake.'

Constance looked at the table. There were tinned peaches and tinned pears, little cakes, plates of brown and white bread-and-butter, and a plate of tartlets. What Constance did not know was with this layout the family had starved themselves for a month.

'What a spread,' said Constance. 'It takes one's breath away.'

'Well 'ow do you think Mr Seivers is lookin'?' asked Mrs Tewson.

Seivers was his new name, he had finished with Soames. They were foster parents.

'Oh! – Not well, not very well,' said Constance hastily to get it over with. 'Can't he do anything else – something lighter, like taking round the tea trolley?' said Constance.

'I'm goin' t'ave another go at Mr Fellows to get im in th' tool shed. That's the place for 'im. It's not heavy work, stamping EPNS on the cutlery,' said Bill. 'But he'll have to wear a truss.'

'Wouldn't they if you paid them? If you said:

Here's five pounds, or ten, if you'll get Soames into the tool shed!' said Constance.

A slow smile spread over Bill's face. 'Well, I've never 'ad five or ten pounds to try 'im with.'

'Then can't you hand him five pounds, or what he wants, from a friend of Soames?' said Constance.

'Wait while I feel my way, an' I'll let you know,' said Bill. 'I wouldn't do it for anybody but Oliver, especially as he was in France with me. He stood in front of me and stopped a shell from hitting me, it hit his cigarette case.'

Soames came in with his face washed and pinched. Why oh why had he been in the scullery pinching his face?

Soames used his knife and fork clumsily with swollen hands and was silent.

'Bill,' said Mrs Tewson. 'Can't you see to that child! Marjory-love, not on mother's clean table-cloth! No!'

Marjory-love was reaching over and spooning a mixture of tea and fruit juice on to the table-cloth.

'Draw her back a bit from th' table!' said her mother.

Marjory-love, drawn back from the table, made pools of tea on her tray, and splashed them with her chubby fists, so that the drops flew among the guest, especially the guest Lady Chatterley.

Bill removed the tea and slopped food from the child's tray. Marjory-love, without a sound, sent her spoon flying across the table where it hit Soames on the back of his head.

'Ere! Ta'e that, an' be good!' said Bill, giving the child a lemon-curd tart. She immediately squashed it up into a mess, and demanded water-cress. He gave Marjory-love the water-cress.

'She's a bonny child!' said Constance.

Marjory-love threw a jam tart which hit Constance in the eye. 'So this was the working class,' thought Constance.

Mrs Tewson took Marjory-love by the throat and shook her like a rag doll.

'You must eat, my lady, or we s'll think it's not good enough for yer,' said Mrs Tewson.

She could feel Soames inwardly squirming, at her elbow. He was eating tinned peaches and thickened cream like a pig.

'How are yer gettin' on at Tevershall, like?' said Bill. 'I've been over there. I stopped a night in th' cottage wi' Oliver – didn't I lad?'

'Really! I didn't see you,' said Constance.

'No! But I seed you an' Sir Clifford in th' park. – You didn't know Oliver so well at that time, like.'

'It was raisin' the young pheasants this spring as started you talkin' to me a bit,' said Oliver, cold and quiet, turning to her. She looked at him, and saw he resented their knowing much of his relationship with her, least of all as he was screwing her.

'Do you mind,' said Bill, 'if I asked you a question, a plain question?' He went on eating peaches and cream, the cream settling on his moustache like frost.

'Not at all,' said Constance.

'Well, what I want to know – Do you think it is

possible for people in a very different walk of life to be friends – really friends?'

'I don't think you can generalize,' said Constance. 'If you mean me and Soames, I think we're quite good friends.'

Good friends? At this moment he was wearing her nightdress inside his underpants.

Bill leaned forward and stared hard at Constance.

'Could you not stare so hard at me,' she said.

'If I had been brought up and eddicated like Sir Clifford, for example – I should be about as good a man as he is,' said Bill.

'Yes, no doubt,' she said. 'I don't think real difference goes by class.'

'What's the good o' talkin' about it!' said Soames testily. 'Leave it alone! It's gettin' yer face all squanged.'

Constance had had enough.

''Ave a drop more tea now!' said Mrs Tewson. 'I've got 'alf a potful.'

She could leave it there, thought Constance.

'I really must go,' said Constance rising, wiping the remnants of jam tart off her face.

'Oh, Oliver'll go with you,' said Bill.

'Perhaps he doesn't want to be bothered,' she said, turning to look at him.

'If you'll wait a minute for me!' he replied, and he went upstairs.

'Well!' said Bill, rising and stretching himself, adding five inches to his height. 'It has been nice havin' a talk with somebody from above.'

'From above? You must be mistaking me for some-body in a tree,' said Constance.

He came downstairs, and in silence they departed, walking side by side down the steep stone slant of the hideous street. He looked a poor little working-man and she knew he felt it. He did, every night in fact.

In the tram-car he sat silent, with his damaged hands curled against his body for comfort. Only he, being the man, got the pennies out of his trousers' pocket, screaming with pain as he did. Constance looked at the depressing ugliness of the other passen-gers, poorish working class, without colour, grace or form, or even warmth of life. It was too gruesome. Yes, the working class looked bloody awful. She had just been to tea with some and they were bloody awful.

Chapter XXIV

THE NEXT DAY she had a letter from him, not so very badly written. – 'Bill told me about your bribing Fellows to get me in the toolshop. Don't do it. I'm leaving anyhow. I knew what you were thinking, Tuesday. So I went to give my notice in this morning, and they are letting me off on Saturday. So I shall look around for something else, an Assistant Bank Manager. I shall go around the country and try and get some farm-labouring. I ought to find some with the corn harvest coming on. I can't go far because of my divorce hanging over me but I will give up trying to work with a lot of other chaps. I can't stomach it. I have to be doing something where I can be by myself. [What was wrong with being a lighthouse keeper?] If I get a farm-labourer's job, I shan't get more than thirty shillings a week, so my mother will have to come down and help me pull the plough. I don't seem to be much use on the face of the earth. ['Then why not try the back,' thought Constance]. I feel I can't breathe easy with other folks.' So being in the vicinity of other people restricted his breathing.

She wrote to him saying, 'I want to tell you that I have decided I must leave Clifford. He will, of course, attempt to commit suicide and I will do everything I can to make it easy for him. I feel I am living here under false pretences. This morning I felt I was Zai Ping, the Empress of China. I looked in the mirror and I wasn't, thank heavens. I mean would you want to go on seeing me as the Empress Zai Ping of China? It's not really on your account. [He didn't have an account — he was skint.] I am sorry for Clifford. He doesn't really want me, except for doing the Charleston nude. But we must think of our child. I should like you to be its father and I should like to be its mother. People have no freshness in their souls. You still have some, if it isn't soon killed off.'

He had no intention of having the freshness of his soul killed off. He always washed under his arms.

He replied to her letter by return, writing with a spanner in the Mechanics Hall.

'I'm sorry you feel that way about Wragby. You would be homeless if you go. Shall you go to Canada with me! I will go next week if you will. I've a cousin there as would help me. He lives on a reservation and sticks feathers in his hair.'

By return, he had her answer.

'I'm so glad you are leaving Sheffield. I was so afraid you were just going to deteriorate into a socialist or fascist, or something dreary like a duck. Shall we meet at Hucknall Church on Sunday?'

They both had their letters on Friday. He wrote:

'I wanted not to say things in a letter. But if you don't feel certain, I'll tell you. I really don't know what love is. I think it's fucking. If a man starts thinking, the fat is in the fire. Everything is a prison, I know that. You are home to me and I don't care about houses. Maybe because I haven't got one. Everything is a prison. Yes, an elephant is a prison if you are inside one. I'll wait by Hucknall church out of sight of Field so he shan't see me. And tell him to meet you again at Annessley lodge gates, by the hall. But if you change it, I shall bide by what you say.'

She knew what it meant – it meant the wood where she had been in stillness with Soames. It meant the fullness of life that trees have, which never want to wander away to somewhere else. How did she know? Many trees wanted to move but didn't know how to do it.

She walked into the dreary sort of Square where the church of Hucknall stands so distinguished, holding the heart of the seething Byron, who had no peace. 'There's not a joy the world can give like that it takes away!' Why do poets say these things, and then not be true to the joy the world can only destroy, if you let it? They hoped to be a poet rather like William McGonagall.

Oh wonderful Hucknall
Let us hope the steeple will never fall
They say Byron's heart is buried there
But some people look and say where.

Soames came forward to meet her, taking off his hat. She looked at him almost in dread. His face was still pale and pinched. Why did he keep on pinching it? It had been as if a wire net was pulled over it making a series of squares on his face.

They went into the dark church together and looked at the little slab behind which rests the pinch of dust which was Byron's heart: in that thrice-dismal Hucknall Torkard. The sense of the greatness of human mistakes made her want to cry.

He was very still and she didn't know what he was thinking, but actually he was thinking of screwing her. She groped for his hand, and it closed over hers. While she held it in both her hands, clinging to it for safety, she fell off the pew.

'You *mustn't* go away from me!' she whispered pathetically.

At that very moment he was trying to work out how he could get away from her without her noticing.

She put both her hands over his hand, and peace began to come into her again, in the dark church, where is the pinch of dust that was Byron's heart.

Soames looked but couldn't see anything. 'Where?' he said echoing William McGonagall's words.

'You must help me to get out,' she said.

'You'll need a removal van,' he said. 'What would you like me to do?'

He was perfectly still. She never knew what he thought. Actually he wasn't thinking of anything.

'You don't want to go to Canada, do you?' he said. 'Nor Australia, nor Africa?'

She suddenly rose and undressed and before they knew what they were doing, like Abélard and Héloïse they were screwing in the aisle and worshippers had to step over them. The vicar tapped him on the shoulder. 'Do you mind?'

'Take me somewhere where you can hold me in your arms!' she said.

'How about Canada, Australia or Africa,' he said.

So he took a footpath towards Felley Mill and in spite of the risk of gamekeepers sending them away, they went into a little hollow of wood, hidden behind the great bramble and rose-bushes.

'I must touch you! I must touch you, or I shall die!' she said.

To save her from death, he let her touch him.

'Ay! Touch me then!' he said quietly, saving her from death, unfastening the front of his trousers and pulling away the shirt from his body. She slipped her arms round his naked waist, curling her face against his belly, and he put his hands under her, until he found her naked body. All the time it had been inside the dress.

'Oh, hold me! Hold me!' she moaned. And he drew her a little closer. Till his hands seemed to go to sleep on her naked body, and she dozed in peace. It was some accomplishment to fall asleep while you were being screwed. And once more her womb was soft with peace and that queer, sap-like happiness over which one has no control. And he was the sap who was going to be the father.

His quick ears (they did thirty miles per hour) were startled by a sound. He looked up, and saw a keeper, a big-faced, middle-aged man, striding round the brambles and dog-rose thickets. Quickly he put her dress down, and as she began to lift her face he murmured:

'Keep still! There's keeper! Dunna move!' And he held her closer.

'Now then!' said the burly keeper, in ugly challenge, and Soames felt all her body jolt in his arms. He pressed her closer. The keeper was smiling an ugly smile.

'Let us be, man, can't you!' said Soames, in a soft, quiet voice, looking into the light-blue, half-triumphant eyes of the other fellow. 'We're harmin' nothing. Have yer niver 'ad a woman in your arms yourself!' The perfect quiet rebuke of his voice was in key with the steady, unabashed rebuke in his eyes. But he remained still and defenceless, his clothing all undone and hanging out, with an erection that was starting to wilt the longer the keeper kept him there, the woman hiding her face against his naked body, under his turned-back shirt.

The keeper looked at the clinging woman hiding her face, and at her legs in their silk stockings. He slowly looked away, and the nasty smile went off his face.

'Aye!' he said, in a changed voice. 'But Squire an' some of 'is folks is walkin' a bit down the 'coppy and they don't want to see that,' he said indicating the erection.

'They aren't comin' this road, are they? Nobody can see us in here,' said Soames.

'You won't stop long, though,' said the keeper and walked off.

'You can't go anywhere for a good fuck,' said Soames. 'Niver mind, 'e's gone! Dunna bother about it, it's nawt, 'e's not a bad sort of chap. What's it matter! What's it matter! There's folks ivrywhere! I'm a folk and I'm everywhere.'

'I know the old squire here,' said Constance.

And she rose, and they went slowly back to the path where long ago Byron must have limped with his wonky leg in his unhappy inability to feel sure in his love. Had he been interrupted by a gamekeeper as he was about to orgasm? All that and a gammy leg.

The old, old countryside where Byron walked, limping along behind Mary Chaworth.

'If I really want you to do something, will you do it?' Constance asked.

'Anything except pulling a plough.'

'If I can't bear it will you come and live with me, even next month. We can go to Italy.'

'Oh! How about Canada, Australia or South Africa?'

'If you feel that's better, I will.'

She kissed him and walked up the street.

He went to cross the road and was run over by a bus.